2

CAHIER

An Intermediate

Workbook for

Grammar and

Communication

David M. Stillman, Ph.D.
Ronni L. Gordon, Ph.D.

National Textbook Company
a division of NTC/CONTEMPORARY PUBLISHING GROUP
Lincolnwood, Illinois USA

Editorial Development: Mediatheque Publishers Services, Philadelphia, Pennsylvania

ISBN: 0-8442-1442-6

Published by National Textbook Company,
a division of NTC/Contemporary Publishing Group, Inc.,
4255 West Touhy Avenue,
Lincolnwood (Chicago), Illinois 60646-1975 U.S.A.
© 1999 NTC/Contemporary Publishing Group, Inc.
Manufactured in the United States of America.

890 VL 0987654321

CONTENTS

Preface   **iv**

1. -**Er** Verbs; -**Er** Verbs with Spelling Changes   **1**

2. -**Ir** Verbs; -**Re** Verbs   **12**

3. Irregular -**Ir** Verbs   **21**

4. Irregular Verbs: **avoir, être, faire, savoir, connaître**   **31**

5. Irregular Verbs: **aller, vouloir, pouvoir, devoir, venir**   **45**

6. Irregular Verbs: **prendre, mettre, lire, écrire, croire, voir, dire, rire, suivre, recevoir**   **58**

7. Gender and Number of Nouns; Definite, Indefinite, and Partitive Articles; **C'est** *versus* **il est**   **72**

8. Adjectives: Forms, Position, Comparative, Superlative   **87**

9. Question Formation   **101**

10. Negative Expressions and Indefinite Adjectives and Pronouns   **111**

11. Object Pronouns   **124**

12. The **passé composé**   **138**

13. The Imperfect; Imperfect *versus* **passé composé**   **149**

14. Commands (The Imperative)   **160**

15. Reflexive Verbs   **169**

16. Relative Clauses   **180**

17. Adverbs   **189**

18. Review of Prepositions; Geographical Names   **198**

19. The Future and the Conditional   **207**

20. The Present Subjunctive   **217**

End Vocabulary: French-English   **227**

Index   **235**

PREFACE

Cahier 2: An Intermediate Workbook for Grammar and Communication is designed to provide second-year learners of French with the tools necessary to consolidate what they have learned, review and practice key topics covered in second year, and lay a solid foundation for advanced study. Organized into 20 chapters, *Cahier 2* presents concise and well-organized **grammar explanations** with clear illustrative examples. The **exercises** in *Cahier 2* give learners of French ample review of basic structures, especially verb forms, and provide varied practice of the patterns presented in most second-year textbooks. *Cahier 2* keeps communicative goals central by offering students contextualized practice of structures to help them build accuracy and confidence. **Vocabulary** sections review and expand upon the vocabulary presented in first-year basal texts. *Cahier 2* highlights important aspects of the French-speaking world in the **cultural notes;** these cultural topics are integrated into culture boxes that help create an authentic context for the exercises as well. Culture topics presented include the French school system, vacations, climate, geography, historical figures, the Louvre museum, car manufacturing, and the Francophone world.

Progressing from structured practice to self-expression, *Cahier 2* offers **Questions personnelles** and **Compositions,** thus encouraging learners to use the grammatical structures and the vocabulary they have studied to express their own ideas. Learners and teachers can evaluate mastery of grammatical points by using the two comprehensive **Progress Checks** provided in the *Answer Key: Progress Check 1* for chapters 1-10; *Progress Check 2* for chapters 11-20.

Students will find working through *Cahier 2* pleasant and rewarding because of its easy-to-follow format, the ample space provided to write answers, its clear and practical presentation of grammar, and its open and inviting design. Teachers will appreciate the flexible organization of *Cahier 2,* which allows them to use chapters in any order to reinforce the grammar points they are presenting in their classes. The unique integration of all its features makes *Cahier 2* an engaging workbook that will motivate learners to communicate and help them build confidence as they master increasingly more complex structures in French. A student-centered, communicative approach makes *Cahier 2* the perfect companion for every second-year textbook.

-Er Verbs;
-Er Verbs with Spelling Changes

I. Regular verbs ending in *-er*

■   -**Er** verbs are conjugated like **parler**:

PARLER *(TO SPEAK)*

singular		plural	
je parl**e**	*I speak*	nous parl**ons**	*we speak*
tu parl**es**	*you speak*	vous parl**ez**	*you speak*
il/elle parl**e**	*he, she, it speaks*	ils/elles parl**ent**	*they speak*
on parl**e**	*people, they, we speak*		

Notes:

1. If the verb begins with a vowel or a mute **h,*** then **je** becomes **j'**, as in **j'arrive, j'habite, j'hésite.**

2. The subject pronoun **on** refers to people in general or to a nonspecific subject. It has various equivalents in English.

Ici **on** parle français.	*French is spoken here.*
On ferme la boutique à midi.	*The shop is closed at noon.*
On entre par là.	*You go in over there./The entrance is over there.*

In colloquial language, **on** sometimes means *we.*

On joue au football cet après-midi.	*We're playing soccer this afternoon.*
On invite Michèle?	*Are we inviting Michèle?*

3. The present tense of French verbs can be translated into English in several different ways.

Nous parlons français.	***We speak*** *French. We are speaking French.*

In questions, English *do* or *does* is not translated in French.

Parles-tu espagnol?	***Do you speak*** *Spanish?*

---

*The letter **h** is silent in French. With a few exceptions, words that begin with **h** are treated as if they begin with a vowel.

■ Some common -er verbs:

accepter *to accept*

accompagner *to accompany*

adorer *to adore, to love*

aider *to help*

aimer *to like, to love*

apporter *to bring*

apprécier *to value, to rate highly; to appreciate*

arrêter *to stop*

arriver *to arrive*

bavarder *to chat*

casser *to break*

cesser *to stop*

chanter *to sing*

chercher *to look for*

continuer *to continue*

danser *to dance*

décider *to decide*

décrocher (le téléphone) *to pick up the phone, to answer the phone*

déjeuner *to have lunch*

demander *to ask, to ask for*

dépenser *to spend (money)*

déposer *to deposit*

dessiner *to draw*

détester *to hate*

deviner *to guess*

dîner *to have dinner*

donner *to give*

écouter *to listen to*

emporter *to carry/take away, to carry off*

emprunter *to borrow*

enseigner *to teach*

entrer *to enter, to come/go in*

étudier *to study*

expliquer *to explain*

fermer *to close*

gagner *to earn, win*

garder *to keep, to watch; to babysit*

habiter *to live (reside)*

hésiter *to hesitate*

inviter *to invite*

jouer *to play*

laisser *to leave behind (used with things); to allow, to let*

laver *to wash*

louer *to rent*

marcher *to walk*

monter *to go up(stairs); to climb*

montrer *to show*

organiser *to organize*

oublier *to forget*

parler *to speak, to talk*

passer *to pass; to spend (time); to take (test)*

penser *to think*

porter *to carry; to wear*

pratiquer *to practice*

préparer *to prepare*

présenter *to present; to introduce*

prêter *to lend*

raccompagner *to walk someone back home, to drive someone home*

raccrocher (le téléphone) *to hang up*

raconter *to tell, to tell about, to relate*

rapporter *to bring back*

refuser *to refuse*

regarder *to look at*

remercier *to thank, to say thank you to*

rencontrer *to meet (by chance)*

rentrer *to return home, to go back*

rester *to stay, to remain*

retourner *to return, to come/go back*

retrouver *to meet (by appointment)*

saluer *to greet*	**travailler** *to work*
sonner *to ring*	**traverser** *to cross*
téléphoner *to phone*	**trouver** *to find*

A. Au lycée. Luc talks about his secondary school. To find out what he says, complete each of the following sentences with the correct present tense form of the verb in parentheses.

1. Dans notre lycée nous _____ *(étudier)* beaucoup.

2. Les étudiants _____ *(passer)* des heures à la bibliothèque.

3. On _____ *(travailler)* dur.

4. Nos professeurs _____ *(enseigner)* très bien.

5. M. Lafarge _____ *(enseigner)* les maths.

6. Il _____ *(expliquer)* les problèmes difficiles.

7. Moi, j'_____ *(étudier)* l'anglais et l'allemand.

8. Toi, tu _____ *(aider)* les étudiants avec l'anglais parce que tu es américain.

9. Marie, Josette, quand est-ce que vous _____ *(passer)* l'examen d'allemand?

10. Demain? Je comprends pourquoi vous _____ *(travailler)* tout le temps.

B. Entre amis. Claude runs into his friends after school. To find out what happens, complete the following story with the correct present tense forms of the verbs in parentheses.

1. Je _____ *(rencontrer)* mes copains après le lycée.

2. Je _____ *(saluer)* tout le monde.

3. Nous _____ *(bavarder)* ensemble.

4. Odile et Chantal _____ *(organiser)* une surboum pour samedi soir.

5. Elles _____ *(inviter)* tout le monde.

6. Nous _____ *(remercier)* les deux filles.

7. Jacques n'_____ pas *(accepter)* l'invitation. Il est pris *(busy)* samedi.

8. Mais moi, j'_____ *(accepter)*. J'aime les surboums.

La scolarité en France

- The French educational system is organized as follows:
  la maternelle *nursery school*
  l'école primaire *elementary school (five years)*
  le collège *middle school (three years)*
  le lycée *high school (three years)*
- Schooling is compulsory until the age of 16. There are both academic and technical lycées in France, and students are assigned to one or the other according to their abilities and interests. For admission to universities, students must pass the very rigorous **baccalauréat,** an examination given during their final year at the **lycée.**

C. Entre amies. How does Véronique help her friends Claudette and Danielle who are studying so hard? Find out by completing the following story with the correct present tense forms of the verbs in parentheses.

Le téléphone _____ (1. *sonner*). Je _____

(2. *décrocher*). C'est mon amie Claudette qui _____

(3. *téléphoner*). Nous _____ (4. *bavarder*) un peu.

Elle _____ (5. *étudier*) avec Danielle. Elles _____

(6. *travailler*) dur. Je dis: «Vous _____ (7. *travailler*) trop.

Venez au café. Je vous _____ (8. *inviter*)!» Claudette et Danielle

_____ (9. *accepter*) mon invitation. Nous _____

(10. *raccrocher*). Je _____ (11. *retrouver*) mes amies devant

le café. Nous _____ (12. *chercher*) une table et nous

_____ (13. *bavarder*). Nous _____ (14. *passer*)

deux heures ensemble.

D. Parlons un peu de vous. Write your opinions about these things using the verbs **adorer, aimer, détester.**

Modèle   <u>J'aime</u> ma maison.

1. _____ les frites.   5. _____ le café.

2. _____ l'école.   6. _____ le chocolat.

3. _____ les légumes.   7. _____ les voitures.

4. _____ les sports.   8. _____ les examens.

E. Samedi soir chez les Cauville. Marguerite Cauville tells what each member of her family and their guests are doing this evening. Write the appropriate present tense form of a logical verb from the list below in the space provided.

chanter	écouter	laisser	préparer
danser	jouer	porter	regarder

1. Maman _____ le dîner.

2. Grand-père _____ la télé.

3. Mon frère _____ un message pour son ami Véronique.

4. Ma sœur et son amie Ghislaine _____ aux dames.

5. Mon frère et moi, nous _____ des cassettes.

6. Moi, je _____ une nouvelle jupe.

7. Je _____ avec mon petit ami Robert.

8. Nous _____ la nouvelle chanson.

F. Les actions. Select verbs from the list below that logically complete these conversations and write them in their correct present tense forms in the spaces provided.

chanter	dîner	jouer	louer
dépenser	gagner	laver	pratiquer

1. —Ce soir nous _____ au restaurant «Assiette d'or».

   —C'est vrai? On _____ beaucoup d'argent dans ce restaurant.

2. —Nous _____ un film pour cet après-midi?

   —Pour ce soir peut-être. Cet après-midi je _____ la voiture.

3. —Vous _____ souvent au football?

   —Oui, et nous _____ toujours les matchs.

4. —Tu _____ dans la chorale?

   —Oui, et je _____ des sports aussi.

G. Aussi. Say that the people indicated do these things too. You'll need stressed pronouns for contrast in many cases.

STRESSED PRONOUNS

singular		plural	
moi	*me*	**nous**	*we, us*
toi	*you*	**vous**	*you*
lui	*he, him*	**eux**	*they, them*
elle	*she, her*	**elles**	*they, them*

Modèle Moi, je rentre en voiture. *(toi)*
> ➤ Toi, tu rentres en voiture aussi.

1. Monique arrête de travailler à huit heures. *(Raoul et Sylvie)*

   _____

2. Nous, nous marchons lentement. *(eux)*

   _____

3. M. Dufau enseigne les maths. *(vous)*

   _____

4. Moi, j'organise une surboum. *(toi)*

   _____

5. Eux, ils dépensent beaucoup d'argent. *(nous)*

   _____

6. Mon père continue à travailler. *(mes oncles)*

   _____

7. Lucie garde sa petite sœur. *(Yvette)*

   _____

8. Lui, il raconte des histoires. *(toi)*

   _____

II. *-Er* verbs with Spelling Changes

■ **-Er** verbs whose stems end in **-c, -g,** or **-y** have spelling changes in the present tense. (The stem of a verb is found by dropping the infinitive ending: **-er, -ir, -re,** etc.)

- Verbs whose stems end in -c, such as **commencer** *(to begin)*, add a cedilla under the c (**ç**) in the **nous** form: **nous commençons.** The rest of the conjugation is regular.

- Verbs whose stems end in -g, such as **manger** *(to eat)*, add an -e after the g in the **nous** form: **nous mangeons.** The rest of the conjugation is regular.

- Verbs whose stems end in -y, such as **employer** *(to use)*, change the y to i before a silent **e** (in all the singular forms and in the **ils/elles** form).

EMPLOYER *(TO USE)*

je emploie	nous employons
tu emploies	vous employez
il/elle/on emploie	ils/elles emploient

- Some common verbs whose stems end in -c (c ➤ ç in the **nous** form):

annoncer *to announce*	**menacer** *to threaten*
avancer *to advance*	**placer** *to place; to invest*
commencer *to begin*	**prononcer** *to pronounce*
effacer *to erase*	**remplacer** *to replace*
lancer *to launch*	**renoncer** *to resign, to quit*

- Some common verbs whose stems end in -g (g ➤ ge in the **nous** form):

arranger *to arrange*	**loger** *to house, to put someone up*
changer *to change*	**longer** *to walk along, to go along*
corriger *to correct*	**manger** *to eat*
décourager *to discourage*	**nager** *to swim*
déménager *to move (change residence)*	**partager** *to share*
déranger *to bother, disturb*	**plonger** *to dive*
diriger *to direct*	**ranger** *to put away*
encourager *to encourage*	**rédiger** *to draft, to write*
engager *to hire*	**voyager** *to travel*

- Some common verbs whose stems end in -y (y ➤ i before an ending with a mute **e**):

appuyer *to support*	**essuyer** *to wipe*
balayer *to sweep*	**nettoyer** *to clean*
effrayer *to frighten*	**noyer** *to drown*
employer *to use*	**payer** *to pay*
ennuyer *to bore*	**rayer** *to cross out*
envoyer *to send*	**tutoyer** *to address someone as* **tu**
essayer *to try, to try on*	**vouvoyer** *to address someone as* **vous**

H. Les invités arrivent! Company's coming so the whole family is rushing to straighten up the house. Tell what each person is doing by filling in the correct present tense form of the verbs in parentheses.

1. *(manger)*   Nous _____ vite.

2. *(nettoyer)*   Ma sœur _____ la cuisine.

3. *(ranger)*   Ma frère et moi, nous _____ nos livres.

4. *(balayer)*   Mon père _____ le salon.

5. *(commencer)*   Ma sœur et moi, nous _____ à préparer le café.

6. *(essuyer)*   Mes grands-parents _____ les verres et les tasses.

7. *(arranger)*   Ma mère et moi, nous _____ les fleurs sur la table.

8. *(essayer)*   Notre chien _____ d'aider tout le monde!

I. Le travail des professeurs de français. M. Leclerc is explaining to parents what he and his colleagues in the French department do. Write what he says to them using the **nous** form of the verbs given.

Modèle   enseigner tous les jours
       ➤ Nous enseignons tous les jours.

1. employer le français en classe

   _____

2. tutoyer les étudiants

   _____

3. corriger les compositions

   _____

4. changer le programme cette année

   _____

5. commencer à lire *La Peste**

   _____

6. encourager les étudiants

   _____

*La Peste *(The Plague)* is a widely read novel by Albert Camus (1913–1960), an Algerian-born French writer famous for his existentialist novels.

7. prononcer clairement

_____

8. annoncer les examens à l'avance

_____

III. Other Spelling Changes in *-er* Verbs

■ The stem vowel of the verb **acheter** is a mute **e**. (The **e** is not pronounced.) This **e** is pronounced, however, in all the singular forms and in the **ils/elles** form of the present tense. This pronunciation change is reflected in the spelling: **e** is written **è** in those forms. Study the following conjugation.

ACHETER *(TO BUY)*

j'achète	nous achetons *(mute e)*
tu achètes	vous achetez *(mute e)*
il/elle/on achète	ils/elles achètent

■ The verb **enlever** *(to remove, to take off)* is conjugated like **acheter**: **j'enlève, tu enlèves,** etc. The verbs **appeler** *(to call)* and **jeter** *(to throw)* represent the sound change by doubling the final consonant of the stem in the four affected forms.

APPELER *(TO CALL)*

j'appelle	nous appelons *(mute e)*
tu appelles	vous appelez *(mute e)*
il/elle/on appelle	ils/elles appellent

JETER *(TO THROW)*

je jette	nous jetons *(mute e)*
tu jettes	vous jetez *(mute e)*
il/elle/on jette	ils/elles jettent

■ The verbs **épeler** *(to spell)* and **rappeler** *(to call back)* are conjugated like **appeler.** The verb **rejeter** *(to reject)* is conjugated like **jeter.**

■ Verbs like **espérer** *(to hope)* and **préférer** *(to prefer)* which have the accented vowel **é** in the stem, change **é** to **è** before an ending beginning with a mute **e.**

ESPÉRER *(TO HOPE)*

je espère	nous espérons
tu espères	vous espérez
il/elle/on espère	ils/elles espèrent

PRÉFÉRER *(TO PREFER)*

je préfère	nous préférons
tu préfères	vous préférez
il/elle/on préfère	ils/elles préfèrent

■ The verbs **compléter** *(to complete)* and **répéter** *(to repeat)* are conjugated like **espérer** and **préférer.**

J. **Des questions pour un copain.** Rewrite these questions in the **tu** form as if you were asking them of a friend. Change other words such as possessive adjectives accordingly.

À l'école

la **cantine** *student lunchroom*

le **copain** *(masc.) pal, buddy, friend*

la **copine** *(fem.) pal, buddy, friend*

la **corbeille** *wastebasket*

les **devoirs** *homework*

le **jus de fruits** *fruit juice*

la **matière** *school subject*

la **note** *grade (on a school assignment)*

le **programme d'études** *syllabus*

---

1. Qu'est-ce que vous préférez, l'histoire ou la littérature?

   _____

2. Est-ce que vous espérez recevoir de bonnes notes?

   _____

3. Comment est-ce que vous épelez votre nom?

   _____

4. Est-ce que vous jetez les papiers à la corbeille?

   _____

5. Est-ce vous appelez vos amis tous les jours?

   _____

6. Où est-ce que vous achetez vos vêtements?

   _____

K. Entre étudiants. Paul is telling a new student about the lycée. Rewrite what he says, replacing **nous** with **on** to reflect everyday French speech.

1. Nous préférons manger à la cantine.

   _____

2. Nous achetons un sandwich et un jus de fruits.

   _____

3. Nous jetons nos papiers à la corbeille après le déjeuner.

   _____

4. Nous appelons les copains si les devoirs sont difficiles.

   _____

5. Nous répétons le vocabulaire dans la classe d'allemand.

   _____

6. Nous complétons le programme d'études dans chaque matière.

   _____

L. Composition. Write a composition of eight to ten sentences about your school, what you study, what you and your friends do after school and what you think of the classes and teachers. Incorporate as many **-er** verbs as possible.

-Ir Verbs; -Re Verbs

I. -Ir Verbs

- -Ir verbs are conjugated like **finir**:

FINIR *(TO FINISH)*

je finis	nous finiss**ons**
tu finis	vous finiss**ez**
il/elle finit	ils/elles finiss**ent**
on finit	

- Some common -**ir** verbs:

applaudir *to applaud*	**guérir** *to cure, to make better*
avertir *to warn*	**maigrir** *to get thin*
bâtir *to build*	**mincir** *to get thin*
choisir *to choose*	**obéir** *to obey*
désobéir *to disobey*	**réfléchir** *to think, to reflect on*
établir *to establish*	**remplir** *to fill*
finir *to finish*	**réussir** *to succeed*
fournir *to supply, to provide*	**rougir** *to blush*
grandir *to grow, to grow up*	**salir** *to make dirty*
grossir *to get fat*	**vieillir** *to age, to get old*

A. Les verbes. Write the meaning of each adjective or noun and the -**ir** verb related to it. Write the definition of the verbs, too.

	definition	*verb*	*definition*
1. plein	_____	_____	_____
2. fin	_____	_____	_____
3. gros	_____	_____	_____
4. mince	_____	_____	_____
5. vieux	_____	_____	_____
6. grand	_____	_____	_____
7. rouge	_____	_____	_____
8. sale	_____	_____	_____

B. Quel travail! Everyone's finishing up work before the winter break. Complete each of the following sentences with the correct form of **finir** to find out what these students are working on.

Le travail scolaire	
le dessin *drawing*	**le projet d'études** *project*
la dissertation *essay*	**le roman** *novel*
l'exercice *(masc.) exercise*	**la thèse** *thesis*
la lecture *reading*	**la traduction** *translation*

1. Marc et Jacques _____ leurs devoirs.

2. Moi, je _____ ma dissertation.

3. Robert et Marie _____ leurs dessins.

4. Toi, tu _____ tes exercices.

5. Charles et moi, nous _____ notre projet d'études.

6. Vous, vous _____ vos traductions.

7. Mireille _____ sa thèse.

8. Toute la classe _____ la lecture du roman anglais.

C. Au magasin. Christine and her friends are shopping for clothes for school. Complete these sentences with the correct form of **choisir** to find out what each one has selected.

Au magasin de vêtements	
les baskets *(masc. pl.) sneakers*	**la chemise** *shirt*
le bonnet *woolen hat*	**le chemisier** *blouse*
les chaussettes *(fem. pl.) socks*	**la jupe** *skirt*
les chaussures *(fem. pl.) shoes*	**le pantalon** *pants, pair of pants*

1. Mon amie Solange _____ une jupe.

2. Serge et Guillaume _____ des bonnets pour l'hiver.

3. Moi, je _____ un chemisier.

4. Toi, tu _____ des baskets.

5. Solange et moi, nous _____ des chaussettes.

➤➤➤➤➤

6. Guillaume et toi, vous _____ chaussures.

7. Paulette _____ un pantalon.

8. Frédéric et Charles _____ des chemises.

D. J'aime mon chien. Émilie is talking about her dog. Complete these sentences with the correct form of the verbs in parentheses to find out what her dog is like.

1. Moi j'ai un chien. Il est gentil. Il _____ *(obéir)* presque toujours.

2. Je _____ *(remplir)* son bol quand il veut manger.

3. Il mange bien. Il _____ *(grandir)*.

4. Quand il fait quelque chose de spécial, j'_____ *(applaudir)*. Il aime ça!

5. Un jour mon chien _____ *(réussir)* à entrer dans le salle de séjour.

6. Il _____ *(salir)* le sofa.

7. Ma mère veut savoir pourquoi il _____ *(désobéir)*.

8. «Je crois que notre chien _____ *(vieillir)* un peu, maman.»

II. *-Re* Verbs

■ -Re verbs are conjugated like **vendre**.

VENDRE *(TO SELL)*

je vend**s**	nous vend**ons**
tu vend**s**	vous vend**ez**
il/elle/vend	ils/elles vend**ent**
on vend	

■ -**Re** verbs whose stems do not end in -**d** add a **t** in the third-person singular.

INTERROMPRE *(TO INTERRUPT)*

je interromp**s**	nous interromp**ons**
tu interromp**s**	vous interromp**ez**
il/elle/on interromp**t**	ils/elles interromp**ent**

■ Some useful -**re** verbs:

attendre *to wait for*	**perdre** *to lose*
confondre *to confuse*	**rendre** *to give back, to return*
descendre *to go downstairs, to descend*	**répondre** *to answer*
entendre *to hear*	

E. À perdre. Everyone has something he or she always loses. Use the correct form of the verb **perdre** and the appropriate possessive adjective to find out what each of these people loses.

Modèle Françoise/stylo ➤ Françoise perd toujours son stylo.

> ## Les choses qu'on perd
>
> **le classeur** *loose-leaf binder*   **les lunettes de soleil** *(fem. pl.)*
> **la clé** *key*   *sunglasses*
> **l'écharpe** *(fem.) scarf*   **la montre** *watch, wristwatch*

1. je/cahier

   _____

2. tu/écharpe

   _____

3. mon frère/montre

   _____

4. mes amis/crayons

   _____

5. nous/classeurs

   _____

6. vous/livres

   _____

7. Lise et Jeanne/lunettes de soleil

   _____

8. Maurice/clés

   _____

F. L'attente (Waiting). Each of these people is waiting for someone or something. Use the verb **attendre** to tell whom or what. Remember that **attendre** is followed by a direct object in French.

Modèle sa famille/leur nouvelle voiture
> ➤ Sa famille attend leur nouvelle voiture.

1. les étudiants/l'autobus

   _____

2. les touristes/l'avion

   _____

3. je/le métro

   _____

4. nous/une lettre

   _____

5. vous/le facteur

   _____

6. mes parents/les vacances

   _____

7. tu/le week-end

   _____

8. Claire/le train

   _____

G. Fin d'été. These students have spent the summer in France and have bought a lot of things they don't want to take home. Tell what each one is trying to sell using the verb **vendre.**

Modèle   Jacques/son vélo
        ➤ Jacques vend son vélo.

À vendre

le guide *guidebook*	**le sac de couchage** *sleeping bag*
la mobylette *moped, scooter*	**le sèche-cheveux** *hair-dryer*
le radio-réveil *radio alarm clock*	**la tente** *tent*

---

1. Marc/son guide

   _____

2. Jérôme et moi/nos cartes de France

   _____

3. toi/ta mobylette

   _____

4. moi/mon sac de couchage

   _____

5. Chantal/son radio-réveil

   _____

6. Christine et Véra/leurs sèche-cheveux

   _____

7. vous/vos bicyclettes

   _____

8. Frédéric et Joseph/leur tente

   _____

H. Où descend-on? The verb **descendre** (followed by **dans, à,** or **chez**) can mean *to stay temporarily.* Tell where these people are staying during their vacations.

Modèle   Monique/un hôtel
        ➤ Monique descend dans un hôtel.

Le logement

l'appartement *(masc.) apartment*

l'auberge de jeunesse *(fem.)*
    youth hostel

le château *castle*

le foyer d'étudiants *student house*

le luxe *luxury;*
    de luxe *luxury (adj.)*

meublé *furnished*

le terrain de camping *campsite*

---

1. ma famille/dans un hôtel de luxe

   _____

2. Philippe et son frère/dans un appartement meublé

   _____

3. je/dans un château

   _____

4. tu/dans un foyer d'étudiants

   _____

5. nous/à l'Hôtel France

   _____

6. vous/dans un terrain de camping

   _____

7. Laurent/chez des amis

   _____

8. nos amis/dans une auberge de jeunesse

   _____

Vive les vacances!

For French students there are two main vacations: the long summer vacation (**les grandes vacances**) and the winter break (**les vacances de Noël**) from Christmas to New Year's. For winter vacation, many young people go skiing in the French or Swiss Alps. Other school vacations are **la Toussaint,** a week before and including All Saint's Day on November 1; winter break, two weeks at the end of February; spring break, two weeks in April; and Ascension Day (a Catholic holiday), a week at the end of May. The French school year runs from early September to the end of June.

I. Un professeur sévère. In M. Durand's class students may answer, but they never interrupt. Everyone follows that rule. Say so using the present tense forms of **répondre** and **interrompre.**

Modèle nous ➢ Nous répondons, mais nous n'interrompons pas.

1. Lucien et Claude

   _____

2. je

   _____

3. Marguerite

   _____

4. tu

   _____

5. Sylvie et Janine

   _____

6. Martin

   _____

7. on

   _____

8. vous

   _____

J. Soyons logiques! Complete these sentences with one of the verbs from the chapter that would make sense. Include the verb in its proper present tense form.

1. Tu _____ parce que tu ne manges pas assez.

2. Je passe la journée à nettoyer le salon. Ce chien _____ tout!

3. Les étudiants _____ aux questions du professeur.

4. Nous _____ dans le cours de maths parce que nous étudions beaucoup.

5. Je _____ ma maison parce que je veux déménager.

6. Au magasin tu _____ un cadeau pour ta petite amie.

K. Questions personnelles. Answer these sentences in French.

1. Est-ce tu applaudis au cinéma?

   _____

2. Est-ce que les étudiants interrompent le professeur dans la classe de français?

   _____

3. Est-ce que tu perds souvent tes clés?

   _____

4. Est-ce que tu attends l'autobus pour aller à l'école?

   _____

5. Est-ce que tu finis toujours tes devoirs?

   _____

6. Est-ce que tes amis réussissent dans tous les cours?

   _____

L. Composition. Describe a typical day at school and after school for you and your friends. Write a composition of six to eight sentences, using as many **-ir** and **-re** verbs as you can.

Irregular -Ir Verbs

I.   *-Ir* Verbs Conjugated Like *-er* Verbs

■ A small number of -**ir** verbs are conjugated like -**er** verbs: **ouvrir** *(to open)*, **couvrir** *(to cover)*, **découvrir** *(to discover)*, **offrir** *(to offer)*, and **souffrir** *(to suffer)*.

OUVRIR *(TO OPEN)*

j'ouvre	nous ouvr**ons**
tu ouvr**es**	vous ouvr**ez**
il/elle/on ouvre	ils/elles ouvr**ent**

OFFRIR *(TO OFFER)*

j'offre	nous offr**ons**
tu offr**es**	vous offr**ez**
il/elle/on offre	ils/elles offr**ent**

SOUFFRIR *(TO SUFFER)*

je souffre	nous souffr**ons**
tu souffr**es**	vous souffr**ez**
il/elle/on souffre	ils/elles souffr**ent**

Notes:

1. **Offrir** is used to express *to give something as a gift.*

   Mes parents m'**offrent** des livres   *My parents **give** me books and*
   et des disques compacts pour   *compact discs as birthday gifts.*
   mon anniversaire.

2. **Souffrir de** means *to suffer with* or *from.*

   Il **souffre de** la chaleur.   *He **suffers from** the heat.*

A. On cherche le billet de cent francs. A hundred franc bill has been lost and everyone in the class is frantically looking for it. Tell what each person opens as he or she searches.

Modèle   Jacqueline/l'armoire ➤ Jacqueline ouvre l'armoire.

Des choses à ouvrir	
l'armoire *(masc.) closet*	la serviette *briefcase*
le portefeuille *wallet*	le tiroir *drawer*

1. Marc et Lise/l'armoire

   _____

2. le professeur/sa serviette

   _____

3. moi/la boîte

   _____

4. les étudiants/les tiroirs

   _____

5. nous/nos sacs à dos

   _____

6. toi/ton portefeuille

   _____

7. vous/le dictionnaire

   _____

8. Monique/son sac

   _____

B. Joyeux Noël! Tell what gifts people are giving each other for Christmas using the verb **offrir**.

Modèle   Jean-Paul/collier/sa petite amie Odile
➤ Jean-Paul offre un collier à sa petite amie Odile.

Des cadeaux

l'après-rasage *(masc.) after-shave lotion*

l'argent *(masc.) silver*

le collier *necklace*

le cuir *leather*

le jeu vidéo *video game*

les jumelles *(fem. pl.) binoculars*

les patins à roulettes *(masc. plural) roller skates*

le plateau *tray*

---

1. Michèle/jeux vidéo/son petit frère

_____

2. nous/plateau en argent/nos parents

_____

3. les étudiants/une cassette de chansons françaises/leur professeur de français

_____

4. tu/portefeuille en cuir/ton père

_____

5. je/patins à roulettes/ma petite sœur

_____

6. vous/jumelles/votre cousin Richard

_____

7. Colette/après-rasage/son petit ami Julien

_____

8. Olivier/fleurs/sa mère

_____

C. **Un voisin louche** *(suspicious-looking).* A group of high school students is suspicious of a new neighbor. Use the verb **découvrir** to tell what they discover about him.

Modèle   Véronique/où il travaille
➤ Véronique découvre où il travaille.

Renseignements

la boîte postale *post office box*

le chef *head, boss*

l'espion *(fem.* **espionne***) spy*

le numéro de téléphone *phone number*

le pays d'origine *country of birth, country of origin*

la radio à ondes courtes *short-wave radio*

le réseau d'espions *spy ring*

---

1. Luc/son vrai nom

   _____

2. toi/son pays d'origine

   _____

3. Chantal et Janine/son adresse en Europe

   _____

4. toi et moi/qu'il a une boîte postale

   _____

5. moi/son numéro de téléphone

   _____

6. Christine et toi/qu'il a des amis louches

   _____

7. Alain et Bernard/qu'il écoute la radio à ondes courtes

   _____

8. nous sommes sûrs que nous/le chef d'un réseau d'espions!

   _____

II. *-Ir* Verbs without *-iss* in the Plural

■ These six **-ir** verbs follow a similar conjugation pattern. They have the endings of **-re** verbs in the singular and they do not add the **-iss** in the plural.

PARTIR *(TO LEAVE, TO SET OUT)*

je pars	nous part**ons**
tu pars	vous part**ez**
il/elle/on part	ils/elles part**ent**

SORTIR *(TO GO OUT, EXIT)*

je sors	nous sort**ons**
tu sors	vous sort**ez**
il/elle/on sort	ils/elles sort**ent**

DORMIR *(TO SLEEP)*

je dors	nous dorm**ons**
tu dors	vous dorm**ez**
il/elle/on dort	ils/elles dorm**ent**

MENTIR *(TO LIE)*

je mens	nous ment**ons**
tu mens	vous ment**ez**
il/elle/on ment	ils/elles ment**ent**

SENTIR *(TO FEEL, SMELL)*

je sens	nous sent**ons**
tu sens	vous sent**ez**
il/elle/on sent	ils/elles sent**ent**

SERVIR *(TO SERVE)*

je sers	nous serv**ons**
tu sers	vous serv**ez**
il/elle/on sert	ils/elles serv**ent**

Notes:

1. **Partir** means *to leave* in the sense of *to set out, to begin a trip*.

partir en vacances	***to leave** on vacation*
Le train **part** à huit heures.	*The train **leaves** at eight o'clock.*

   Partir de means *to leave from a place;* **partir pour** *to leave for some place.*

L'avion **part de** Paris.	*The plane **leaves from** Paris.*
Nous **partons pour** le Sénégal.	*We're **leaving for** Senegal.*

2. **Sortir** means *to go out.* It is the opposite of **entrer. Sortir** must be followed by **de** before a noun that expresses place.

Je **sors de** ma chambre.	*I'm **going out** of my room.*

Sortir can mean *to go out* both in the sense of *to leave the house* or *to date*.

Je ne **sors** pas quand il neige.   *I **don't go out** when it snows.*

Mireille **sort** avec Julien.   *Mireille **is going out** with Julien.*

3. **Sentir** often means *to smell*.

Je ne **sens** rien parce que je suis enrhumé.   *I **don't smell** anything because I have a cold.*

La petite fille **sent** les fleurs.   *The little girl **is smelling** the flowers.*

Ça **sent** bon/mauvais.   *That **smells** good/bad.*

D. Dimanche matin à la campagne. Renée describes a beautiful Sunday morning in the country. To find out what it was like, complete the following sentences with the correct form of the verbs in parentheses.

Dans le jardin

l'arbre *(masc.) tree*   **le nid** *nest*

frais *(fem.* **fraîche***) fresh*   **l'oiseau** *(masc.) bird*

le jardin *garden*   *(pl.* **les oiseaux***)*

---

1. Il est huit heures. Nous _____ *(ouvrir)* les fenêtres.

2. Les fleurs du jardin _____ *(sentir)* si bon!

3. J'_____ *(ouvrir)* la porte.

4. Je _____ *(sortir)* avec ma petite sœur Viviane.

5. Viviane _____ *(découvrir)* un nid dans un arbre.

6. Les petits oiseaux _____ *(dormir)* dans le nid.

7. Maman _____ *(servir)* le petit déjeuner dans le jardin.

8. Le pain frais _____ *(sentir)* très bon.

E. Qu'est-ce qu'on mange? What are these people serving this evening? Form sentences using the verb **servir** to find out.

Modèle   je/du café ➤ Je sers du café.

1. ma mère/du poisson

_____

2. tes parents/de la viande

_____

3. nous/des légumes

_____

4. tu/des frites

_____

5. je/du rosbif

_____

6. pour le dessert, on/des bonbons

_____

7. vous/du thé

_____

8. mes copains/des tartes aux fruits

_____

F. Les vacances. Where and when are all these people going on vacation? Form sentences with the verb **partir** to find out.

Modèle   tu/en Italie ➤ Tu pars en Italie.

1. Christine et Sara/en Suisse

_____

2. Jean-Paul/aux États-Unis

_____

3. je/en province

_____

4. tu/pour trois semaines

_____

5. nous/dimanche

_____

➤➤➤➤➤

6. vous/en Afrique

_____

7. vous/la semaine prochaine

_____

8. Marie/avec vous

_____

Le tourisme

France is one of the world's most popular tourist destinations, and within France, Paris is always the favorite city. Over two million Americans visit France every year, as do nearly twelve million Germans and eight million Britons. In addition to Paris, other popular tourist destinations in France are **la Provence** and its Mediterranean coast, the French Alps, and the magnificent castles of the Loire valley.

G. Trop de bruit. These people all keep their windows closed when they sleep because they live on a noisy street. Say so using the verbs **ouvrir** and **dormir.**

Modèle   Marie ➢ Marie n'ouvre pas les fenêtres. Comme ça, elle dort mieux.

1. mes parents

_____

2. tu

_____

3. mon frère

_____

4. vous

_____

5. nous

_____

6. on

_____

7. tu

_____

8. je

_____

H. Tout le monde sort. Use the verb **sortir** to answer these questions. Say in each case that the person asked about is not staying, but going out.

Modèle —Marie reste ici?
➤ —Non, elle sort.

1. —Tu restes ici?

— _____

2. —Bernard et Rachel restent ici?

— _____

3. —Je reste ici, maman?

— _____

4. —Mon frère et moi, nous restons ici?

— _____

5. —Toi et tes copains, vous restez ici?

— _____

6. —Monique reste ici?

— _____

7. —Laurent reste ici?

— _____

8. —Ta mère et ta grand-mère restent ici?

— _____

I. **Expansion.** These people are honest. Say that they never lie, using the verb **mentir** as in the model.

Modèle Jacques est honnête. ➤ Il ne ment jamais.

1. Moi, je suis honnête. _____

2. Toi, tu es honnête. _____

3. Natalie est honnête. _____

4. Suzanne et Zoë sont honnêtes. _____

5. Nous, nous sommes honnêtes. _____

6. Marc est honnête. _____

7. Luc et Paul sont honnêtes. _____

8. Vous, vous êtes honnête. _____

J. **Questions personnelles.** Answer these questions in French.

1. Quand pars-tu en vacances? Pars-tu avec ta famille?

_____

2. Sors-tu toujours le week-end?

_____

3. Qu'est-ce que tu offres à ton meilleur ami (à ta meilleure amie) pour son anniversaire?

_____

4. Qu'est-ce que tes parents t'offrent pour ton anniversaire? Pour Noël?

_____

5. Chez toi, est-ce qu'on ouvre les fenêtres pour dormir?

_____

6. Qu'est-ce que tu sers à tes amis quand ils viennent passer l'après-midi chez toi?

_____

K. **Composition.** Describe the comings and goings of people in a busy restaurant or café. Mention who opens doors, comes in, goes out, what the waiters are serving, etc. Write five to seven sentences.

Irregular Verbs:
avoir, être, faire, savoir, connaître

I. *Avoir* and *être*

■ The two most common irregular verbs in French are **avoir** and **être**.

AVOIR *(TO HAVE)*

j'ai	nous avons
tu as	vous avez
il/elle/on a	ils/elles ont

ÊTRE *(TO BE)*

je suis	nous sommes
tu es	vous êtes
il/elle/on est	ils/elles sont

A. Prêts à faire du sport. A group of students has gotten together on Sunday afternoon. Tell what piece of sports equipment they have using the verb **avoir**.

Modèle   Corinne/son vélo
➤ Corinne a son vélo.

Pour faire du sport

le ballon de foot *soccer ball*

la canne à pêche *fishing rod*

le crosse *hockey stick*

le palet *puck*

les patins à roulettes *(masc.)*
roller skates

la planche à roulettes *skateboard*

la raquette de tennis
tennis racket

les skis *(masc.) skis*

le vélo *bicycle, bike*

le vélo tout terrain (le VTT)
mountain bike

---

1. Jean et Normand/leurs crosses et un palet

_____

2. Suzanne/une raquette de tennis

_____

3. moi/mes skis

_____

4. toi/ton vélo tout terrain

_____

5. mes frères et moi/des cannes à pêche

_____

6. Michel/sa planche à roulettes

_____

7. vous/des patins à roulettes

_____

8. Aimée et Marguerite/un ballon de foot

_____

Les sports

Sports are somewhat different in France than in the U.S.
- Baseball and American football are virtually unknown in France, where the most popular sport is soccer (**le football**). Other popular team sports are rugby, volleyball and basketball.
- Traditionally, the French have preferred individual sports to team sports. The man responsible for the modern Olympic Games, Pierre de Coubertin, was a Frenchman. The prime example of individual sports in France is cycling. The yearly **Tour de France,** a national bicycle race of nearly 2500 kilometers, attracts cyclists from all over the world.
- The French Alps offer many opportunities for sports. Millions of people climb mountains and hike in the summer and ski in the winter.
- Other popular spectator sports in France are horse-racing and auto-racing.

B. Où sont-ils? The following people are at different places in town today. Use the verb **être** to tell where they all are. Remember that the preposition **à** contracts with the definite article **le** to form **au** and with the plural definite article **les** to form **aux**.

Modèle   Lise/à/la bibliothèque
➤ Lise est à la bibliothèque.

La ville

le **grand magasin** *department store*   le **stade** *stadium*
le **musée d'art** *art museum*   le **zoo** *the zoo*
la **piscine** *swimming pool*

---

1. moi/à/piscine

   _____

2. Serge et Marc/à/stade

   _____

3. Janine/à/concert

   _____

4. mes parents/dans/grands magasins

   _____

5. toi/à/musée d'art

   _____

6. vous/à/match

   _____

7. mes sœurs et moi/à/zoo

   _____

8. les copains/à/cinéma

   _____

C. C'est à qui alors? Use the verb **avoir** and the idiom **être à** *(to belong to)* to help Micheline find out whom all the things lying around belong to. Create exchanges in which you tell Micheline that the person she asks about doesn't have the item. End with a stressed pronoun.

STRESSED PRONOUNS

moi	*me*	nous	*we, us*
toi	*you*	vous	*you*
lui	*he/him*	eux	*they, them*
elle	*she/her*	elles	*they, them (fem.)*

Modèle   stylo/Marc ➤
—Le stylo est à Marc?
—Non, il n'a pas de stylo, lui.

1. dictionnaire/toi

   — _____

   — _____

2. billet de train/moi

   — _____

   — _____

3. sac à dos/Christine

   — _____

   — _____

4. disquettes/garçons

   — _____

   — _____

5. cahiers/tes sœurs

   — _____

   — _____

6. raquette de tennis/Luc

   — _____

   — _____

7. cassette/vous deux

— _____

— _____

8. cartes de France/moi et à Odile

— _____

— _____

II. Expressions with *avoir* and *être*

■ Many phrases that in English consist of the verb *to be* + an adjective have French equivalents that consist of the verb **avoir** + a noun.

avoir chaud/froid *to be warm/cold* (said of a person)

avoir faim *to be hungry*

avoir soif *to be thirsty*

avoir sommeil *to be sleepy*

avoir honte (de) *to be ashamed (of)*

avoir peur (de) *to be afraid (of)*

avoir raison *to be right*

avoir tort *to be wrong*

avoir de la chance *to be lucky*

With most of these expressions, **très** is used as an intensifier.

On va manger? J'ai **très** faim.	*Shall we go eat? I'm **very** hungry.*
Les enfants ont **très** sommeil.	*The children are **very** sleepy.*

■ **Avoir** is used to tell how old you are in French.

—Quel âge **as**-tu?	*How old are you?*
—J'**ai** seize ans.	*I'm sixteen.*

■ The expressions **avoir besoin de** *(to need)* and **avoir envie de** *(to want, desire)* require the preposition **de** before a following noun or infinitive.

—Tu **as besoin d'**acheter quelque chose?	*Do you **need** to buy something?*
—Oui, j'**ai besoin d'**un surligneur.	*Yes, I **need** a highlighter.*
—Tu **as envie de** prendre quelque chose?	*Do you **feel like** having something?*
—Oui, j'**ai envie d'**une glace.	*Yes, I **feel like** ice cream.*

■ The expression **avoir mal à** (+ part of the body) is used to tell what hurts.

—Qu'est-ce que tu **as**?	*What's wrong with you? What **hurts** you?*
—J'**ai mal à** la tête.	*I have a headache.*

■ Some expressions with **être**:

être à *to belong to*

être à l'heure *to be on time*

être en retard *to be late*

être en avance *to be early*

être d'accord avec *to agree with*

être de retour *to be back*

être enrhumé(e) *to have a cold*

être en forme *to be in shape, to be physically fit*

être en bonne/mauvaise santé *to be in good/bad health*

être en vacances *to be on vacation*

Note the expression **être en train de faire quelque chose** *(to be in the process of doing something, to be doing something right now).*

Je **suis en train de** faire mes devoirs.   *I'm doing my homework right now.*

D. C'est logique. Circle the correct response or reaction in each of the following cases.

1. Jean fait souvent dix kilomètres à vélo.
   a. Il est enrhumé.
   b. Il a honte.
   c. Il est en forme.

2. Moi, je crois que Yvette a raison.
   a. Tu es d'accord avec elle, alors?
   b. Alors, tu penses qu'elle a tort.
   c. Tu as quel âge, toi?

3. Tu peux venir avec moi au musée?
   a. Non, je suis déjà au musée.
   b. Non, je suis en train de faire mes devoirs.
   c. Non, j'ai de la chance aujourd'hui.

4. Tu as envie de manger quelque chose?
   a. Oui, mais je n'ai pas peur.
   b. Oui, j'ai besoin d'un stylo.
   c. Oui, j'ai très faim.

5. Stéphanie, c'est à toi, cette montre?
   a. Oui, il est dix heures et demie.
   b. Oui, c'est ma montre. Merci.
   c. Oui, mais tu n'as pas de montre.

6. Le prof est fâché contre Philippe?
   a. Oui, parce que Philippe est toujours en retard.
   b. Oui, mais Philippe a soif aussi.
   c. Oui, parce que Philippe est de retour.

7. Ton père ne travaille pas cette semaine?

    a. Non, il est en vacances.

    b. Non, il a sommeil.

    c. Non, il est en avance.

E. Après l'accident. The schoolbus skidded off the road, but luckily no one was seriously hurt. Use the expression **avoir mal à** to tell where each of these students is feeling aches and pains. Remember the contractions **à + le ➤ au** and **à + les ➤ aux.**

Modèle   Christine/épaule ➤ Christine a mal à l'épaule.

Le corps humain	
le bras *arm*	**la jambe** *leg*
le cou *neck*	**la main** *hand*
le dos *back*	**le pied** *foot*
l'épaule *(fem.) shoulder*	**la tête** *head*

1. le chauffeur/tête

    _____

2. moi/pieds

    _____

3. Luc et Charles/dos

    _____

4. toi/cou

    _____

5. Cécile/jambes

    _____

6. toi et moi/mains

    _____

7. vous/bras *(pl.)*

    _____

F. Questions personnelles. Answer the following questions in complete French sentences.

1. Quel âge as-tu?

   _____

2. Est-ce que tu es en vacances maintenant?

   _____

3. Est-ce que tu as souvent soif dans la classe de français?

   _____

4. Est-ce qu'on a chaud ou froid dans la classe de français?

   _____

5. De qui as-tu peur?

   _____

6. Est-ce que tu as envie de voyager en été? Où?

   _____

III. *Faire*

FAIRE *(TO MAKE, TO DO)*

je fais	nous faisons
tu fais	vous faites
il/elle/on fait	ils/elles font

The verb **faire** is used in many expressions in French.

■ **Faire** + **de** + article + school subject means *to take a subject* or, in a university context, *to major in it*. It is used in other expressions related to school.

faire du français *to take French*

faire des maths *to study mathematics*

faire attention (à) *to pay attention (to)*

faire des études *to study (to go to college)*

faire ses devoirs *to do one's homework*

- **Faire** is used to express many common activities and actions, such as household chores.

  faire des achats *to make purchases*

  faire les courses *to do the shopping, especially grocery shopping*

  faire la cuisine *to do the cooking*

  faire le linge, faire la lessive *to do the laundry*

  faire son lit *to make one's bed*

  faire le ménage *to do housework*

  faire la vaisselle *to do the dishes*

- **Faire** is used for many physical activities, especially individual (as opposed to team) sports.

  faire de l'aérobic *to do aerobics*

  faire de l'alpinisme *to go mountain climbing*

  faire de la bicyclette *to go bike riding*

  faire du camping *to go camping*

  faire de l'exercice *to exercise*

  faire du jogging *to go jogging*

  faire de la natation *to go swimming*

  faire du patin à glace *to go ice-skating, to ice-skate*

  faire du patin à roulettes *to go roller-skating, to roller-skate*

  faire de la planche à roulettes *to go skateboarding*

  faire de la planche à voile *to go windsurfing*

  faire de la plongée sous-marine *to go deep-sea diving*

  faire une promenade *to take a walk*

  faire une randonnée *to go on a hike*

  faire du ski *to ski, go skiing*

  faire du ski nautique *to waterski, go waterskiing*

  faire du sport *to play sports*

  faire du tennis *to play tennis*

  faire du vélo *to go bike riding*

  faire de la voile *to go sailing*

- Other activities:

  faire attention à *to pay attention to*

  faire la connaissance de *to meet someone, to get to know someone*

  faire du lèche-vitrine *to go window shopping*

  faire un pique-nique *to have a picnic*

  faire la queue *to stand in line, to wait in line*

faire la sieste *to take a nap*

faire un tour *to take a walk or ride, to have a look around*

faire les valises *to pack (suitcases)*

faire un voyage *to take a trip*

■ Weather expressions:

Quel temps fait-il? *What's the weather?*

Quelle température fait-il? *What's the temperature?*

Il fait beau. *The weather's good.*

Il fait mauvais. *The weather's bad.*

Il fait chaud. *It's hot (outside).*

Il fait froid. *It's cold (outside).*

Il fait du soleil. *It's sunny.*

Il fait du vent. *It's windy.*

Il fait un sale temps. *The weather is lousy.*

Il fait 30 degrés. *It's thirty degrees.*

G. La belle vie. When on vacation these people nap in the afternoon and take a walk in the evening. Say so using the expressions **faire une sieste** and **faire une promenade.**

Modèle Marianne ➤ L'après-midi, Marianne fait une sieste. Le soir, elle fait une promenade.

1. mes parents

   _____

2. je

   _____

3. nous

   _____

4. Luc

   _____

5. tu

   _____

6. vous

   _____

H. L'été. Tell what these people are doing this summer by forming complete sentences with the elements given using the verb **faire** + **de** + article.

Modèle   Claudette/sport ➤ Claudette fait du sport.

1. moi/alpinisme

   _____

2. mon frère Jacquot/patin à roulettes

   _____

3. vous/plongée sous-marine

   _____

4. mes sœurs/camping

   _____

5. Marie et moi/tennis

   _____

6. tes cousins et toi/randonnées

   _____

7. mes parents et moi/voile

   _____

8. toi/ski nautique

   _____

I. Questions personnelles. Answer these questions in a complete French sentence.

1. Quel temps fait-il dans votre région en été?

   _____

2. Quel temps fait-il dans votre région en hiver?

   _____

3. Faites-vous souvent des voyages? Où?

   _____

➤➤➤➤➤

4. Faites-vous du patin ou du ski? (Précisez.)

_____

5. Que faites-vous pour aider vos parents à la maison?

_____

6. Quand vous passez une journée en ville, qu'est-ce que vous faites?
Du lèche-vitrine? des promenades? autre chose?

_____

IV. *Savoir* and *connaître*

SAVOIR *(TO KNOW)*

je sais	nous savons
tu sais	vous savez
il/elle/on sait	ils/elles savent

CONNAÎTRE *(TO KNOW, TO BE FAMILIAR WITH)*

je connais	nous connaissons
tu connais	vous connaissez
il/elle/on connaît	ils/elles connaissent

■ Although **savoir** and **connaître** both mean *to know*, they are used in different ways.

Savoir means *to know a fact* or *an item of information* that you can repeat.

—Tu **sais** le numéro de téléphone de Lise? *Do you know Lise's telephone number?*
—Non, mais je **sais** son adresse. *No, but I know her address.*

Savoir may have a noun as its object, as in the above examples (**le numéro de téléphone, son adresse**) or a sentence. The sentence object is called a dependent or subordinate clause.

—Tu **sais** où Marc habite? *Do you know where Marc lives?*
—Non, mais je **sais** qu'il habite loin d'ici. *No, but I know that he lives far from here.*

When **savoir** is followed by an infinitive it means *to know how do something*.

—Tu **sais** faire du ski nautique? *Do you know how to waterski?*
—Non, mais je **sais** nager. *No, but I know how to swim.*

■ **Connaître** means *to know a person* or *to be familiar with a place*.

—Vous **connaissez** Paris? *Do you know Paris?*
—Oui, et je **connais** une famille à Paris. *Yes, and I know a family in Paris.*

J. Tous ensemble. A group of boys is trying to find out about a new girl at school. They are pooling their information. Form sentences with **savoir** to find out what each knows.

Modèle Luc/qui c'est ➤ Luc sait qui c'est.

1. moi/son adresse

   _____

2. Henri/son téléphone

   _____

3. Philippe et Georges/où elle travaille

   _____

4. toi/quand elle arrive au lycée

   _____

5. nous/quel bus elle prend

   _____

6. vous/à quelle heure elle part

   _____

7. Michel/si elle a un petit ami

   _____

8. moi/son nom

   _____

K. Que savez-vous? Complete the following conversations with the correct forms of **savoir** or **connaître.**

A. —Qui est cet homme?

   —Nous ne _____ (1) pas. Nous ne _____ (2)

pas ce monsieur. Vous pouvez demander à Mme Laurier. Elle

_____ (3) tout le monde.

   —Pardon, Madame.

   —Oui?

➤➤➤➤➤

—Qui est ce monsieur?

—Je ne _____ (4) pas comment il s'appelle. Mais je

_____ (5) que c'est un nouveau professeur.

B. —Pardon, monsieur. Où est le musée d'art?

— Je regrette, mais je ne _____ (6) pas cette ville. Je ne suis

pas d'ici. Je ne _____ (7) pas le musée d'art. Mais voilà un agent

de police. Je suis sûr qu'il _____ (8) où se trouve le musée.

L. **Composition.** Write a paragraph of seven or eight sentences about your favorite leisure time activities and of those of your friends.

Irregular Verbs:
aller, vouloir, pouvoir, devoir, venir

I. *Aller*

ALLER *(TO GO)*

je vais	nous allons
tu vas	vous allez
il/elle/on va	ils/elles vont

■ Expressions with **aller**:

Comment **allez**-vous? *How are you? (formal)*

Comment **ça va**? *How are you? (informal)*

Ça va? *How are you? (informal)*

Je **vais** bien. *I'm all right./I feel okay.*

aller à pied *to walk, go on foot*

aller en voiture *to go by car*

A. Les courses. Use the verb **aller** to tell what store each of these people is going to. Remember the contractions **à** + **le** ➢ **au** and **à** + **les** ➢ **aux**.

Modèle   Madame Laval/l'épicerie
➢ Madame Laval va à l'épicerie.

Les magasins

la boucherie *butcher shop*	**le marché en plein air** *outdoor market*
la boulangerie *bakery*	**la pâtisserie** *pastry shop*
la charcuterie *deli*	**la poissonnerie** *fish store*
la crémerie *dairy, dairy products store*	**le supermarché** *supermarket*
l'épicerie *(fem.) grocery*	

---

1. Aurélie et sa sœur/supermarché

_____

2. moi/boucherie

_____

➢➢➢➢➢➢

3. Jean-Luc/pâtisserie

   _____

4. toi/marché en plein air

   _____

5. vous/boulangerie

   _____

6. nous/charcuterie

   _____

7. Sylvie/poissonnerie

   _____

8. moi/crémerie

   _____

B. **Des courses spécifiques.** Complete these sentences with the correct form of **aller** and the store to which the people indicated would go. Add the preposition à + the definite article or **chez** if the word **marchand** is used.

Modèle Véronique a besoin de pain. Elle <u>va à la boulangerie</u> .

Encore des magasins

les grands magasins *(masc. pl.) department store(s)*
le marchand de fruits *fruit seller*
---

1. Moi, j'ai besoin de viande. Je _____

2. Toi, tu as besoin de vêtements. Tu _____

3. Eux, ils ont besoin d'oranges. Ils _____

4. Paul a besoin de lait. Il _____

5. Nous, nous avons besoin de pain. Nous _____

6. Vous, vous avez besoin d'eau minérale. Vous _____

C. Ils n'y vont jamais. Your friend is surprised that the people indicated are not at these places. You point out that those people never go there. Create dialogs about this with the verbs **être** and **aller** and the negative expression **ne... jamais.**

Modèle   Marc/bibliothèque ➤
        —Marc n'est pas à la bibliothèque.
        —Il ne va jamais à la bibliothèque.

1. tu/stade

  — _____

  — _____

2. Louise/piscine

  — _____

  — _____

3. Philippe et Jacquot/cinéma

  — _____

  — _____

4. je/au bureau

  — _____

  — _____

5. Marie et moi/snack-bar

  — _____

  — _____

6. tu/café

  — _____

  — _____

7. vous/gare

  — _____

  — _____

8. Hervé/plage

  — _____

  — _____

II. The *futur proche*

■ The verb **aller** can be followed by an infinitive and refer to future time. It is similar to the English construction *am/is/are going to do something.*

—Qu'est-ce que vous **allez faire** en été?
*What **are you going to do** in the summer?*

—Nous **allons passer** nos vacances à Paris.
*We're **going to spend** our vacation in Paris.*

D. Je ne sais pas. Your friend is surprised that certain things are not happening. You respond by saying you don't know whether they are going to happen. Use **aller** + infinitive in your answers.

Modèle   Jacques ne mange pas?
➤ Je ne sais pas s'il va manger.

1. Tu ne pars pas?

   _____

2. Alice et Louise ne sortent pas?

   _____

3. Christine ne descend pas?

   _____

4. Nous ne décidons pas?

   _____

5. Vous ne répondez pas?

   _____

6. Pierre ne téléphone pas?

   _____

7. Je ne paie pas?

   _____

8. Tes amis ne déménagent pas?

   _____

E. Voilà ce qu'on va faire. Construct sentences with **aller** + infinitive to tell what these students are going to do this weekend.

Modèle   Luc/dormir
> Luc va dormir.

1. je/faire mes devoirs

   _____

2. Yvette/étudier

   _____

3. Bernard et moi/jouer au football

   _____

4. Marcel/acheter des vêtements

   _____

5. tu/faire de l'exercice

   _____

6. Anne Marie/téléphoner à ses amies

   _____

7. vous/rester à la maison

   _____

8. Ursule et Véra/regarder un film

   _____

III. *Pouvoir, vouloir,* and *devoir*

POUVOIR *(TO BE ABLE TO, CAN)*

je peux	nous pouvons
tu peux	vous pouvez
il/elle/on peut	ils/elles peuvent

VOULOIR *(TO WANT)*

je veux	nous voulons
tu veux	vous voulez
il/elle/on veut	ils/elles veulent

➣➣➣➣➣

DEVOIR *(OUGHT, SHOULD, HAVE TO)*

je dois	nous devons
tu dois	vous devez
il/elle/on doit	ils/elles doivent

Pouvoir, vouloir, and **devoir** can be followed by an infinitive.

—Alain, Claude, vous **voulez aller** au cinéma?

—Nous ne **pouvons** pas **sortir.** Nous **devons finir** les problèmes de maths.

*Alain, Claude, **do** you **want to go** to the movies?*

*We **can't go out.** We **have to finish** the math problems.*

F. **Le moment du dessert.** What do these people want for dessert? Use the correct form of the verb **vouloir** to find out.

Modèle Jean/une tarte aux poires ➤ Jean veut une tarte aux poires.

Les desserts

les bonbons *(masc. pl.) candy*

le chocolat *chocolate*

la crème caramel *caramelized custard dessert*

le fruit *fruit*

le gâteau *cake*

la glace *ice cream*

la mousse au chocolat *chocolate mousse*

la tarte *individual pie-like pastry*

la tarte aux fraises *strawberry pie*

la tarte aux pêches *peach pie*

la tarte aux poires *pear pie*

la tarte aux pommes *apple pie*

---

1. les enfants/du chocolat

   _____

2. moi/du gâteau

   _____

3. toi/une tarte aux fraises

   _____

4. ma mère/de la mousse au chocolat

   _____

5. papa/des bonbons

   _____

6. mes sœurs/des fruits

_____

7. nous/une crème caramel

_____

8. vous/une glace

_____

G. C'est la volonté qui manque *(is missing).* A friend expresses his surprise that people are not doing the things they are supposed to, using a negative question with **pouvoir.** You explain to your friend that it's not that they *can't,* but that they *don't want to.* Notice in the model the use of **Si** instead of **Oui** to answer a negative question.

Modèle Éliane/faire ses devoirs ➤
    —Éliane ne peut pas faire ses devoirs?
    —Si, elle peut, mais elle ne veut pas.

1. Laurent et Michel/nous aider

— _____

— _____

2. tu/préparer le déjeuner

— _____

— _____

3. Marthe/répondre aux questions du professeur

— _____

— _____

4. je/rester à la bibliothèque

— _____

— _____

5. nous/assister au concert de dix-neuf heures

— _____

— _____

➤➤➤➤➤➤

6. le professeur/réviser le vocabulaire

— _____

— _____

7. vous/étudier ce soir

— _____

— _____

8. tu/nettoyer ta chambre

— _____

— _____

L'heure officielle

French uses a 24-hour clock for official purposes such as transportation and entertainment schedules. In this system of telling time **douze heures** replaces **midi** and **vingt-quatre heures** replaces **minuit**. Minutes after the hour are counted from one to fifty-nine, so **et, moins, quart,** and **demie** are not used. The phrases **du matin, de l'après-midi, du soir** and **de la nuit,** which are French equivalents of A.M. and P.M., are also not used in the 24-hour system.

Le film commence à **18h 14.**	*The film begins at 6:14 P.M.*
Le train pour Lyon part à **13h 48.**	*The train for Lyons leaves at 1:48 P.M.*
Bureau fermé entre **12h** et **14h.**	*Office closed between noon and 2 P.M.*

H. Tant de choses à faire. All these people have to turn down invitations because they have to do certain things. Construct dialogs about this using the elements given and the verbs **pouvoir** and **devoir.**

Modèle Françoise/sortir avec nous/étudier ➤
—Françoise peut sortir avec nous?
—Non, elle ne peut pas. Elle doit étudier.

1. Paul/jouer au tennis/garder son petit frère

— _____

— _____

2. tu/manger au restaurant/finir mes devoirs.

— _____

— _____

3. Virginie et Michèle/aller au café/aider leur mère

— _____

— _____

4. je/sortir voir les copains/ranger tes affaires *(belongings)*

— _____

— _____

5. vous/aller au cinéma/faire le ménage

— _____

— _____

6. Suzanne/faire une sieste/préparer le dîner

— _____

— _____

7. nous/faire du lèche-vitrine/nettoyer la cuisine

— _____

— _____

8. je/regarder la télé/descendre acheter du pain

— _____

— _____

I. **Des conseils.** Use the verbs **devoir** (in the negative) and **aller** to express warnings about what can happen if people don't do what they should.

Modèle   Édouard/rester au lit/manquer ton autobus
          ➤ Édouard ne doit pas rester au lit. Il va manquer son autobus.

Attention!

conduire *to drive*

crier *to shout*

la gorge *throat*

les lunettes *(fem. pl.) eyeglasses*

la pluie *rain;* sous la pluie *in the rain*

le rhume *cold;* prendre un rhume *to catch a cold*

tomber *to fall*

---

1. tu/sortir sous la pluie/prendre un rhume

   _____

2. je/faire du jogging quand il pleut/tomber

   _____

3. les enfants/manger tant de bonbons/avoir mal à l'estomac

   _____

4. vous/lire sans vos lunettes/avoir mal aux yeux

   _____

5. nous/crier au stade/avoir mal à la gorge

   _____

6. Olivier/conduire si vite/avoir un accident

   _____

IV. Verbs of Motion + Infinitive

■ Most verbs of motion can be followed directly by an infinitive. The infinitive indicates the purpose for which the person moved or changed places.

—Tu **vas voir** le film?   *Are you **going to see** the movie?*
—Non, je **rentre faire** mes devoirs.   *No, I'm **going back home to do** my homework.*

■ Verbs of motion:

aller *to go*	**passer** *to pass by, to go by*
descendre *to go down, to go downstairs*	**rentrer** *to return, to go home*
entrer *to enter, to go in, to come in*	**revenir** *to come back*
monter *to go up, to go upstairs*	**sortir** *to go out*
partir *to leave*	**venir** *to come*

J. Ce qu'on va faire. Summarize each of the exchanges you see with a sentence consisting of a verb of motion + the infinitive. Follow the model.

Modèle —Marcelle revient?
          —Oui, elle veut voir ses amies.
          ➤ Marcelle revient voir ses amies.

1. —Tu pars?
      —Oui, je dois travailler.

    _____

2. —Richard et Robert passent après?
      —Oui, ils veulent prendre un café avec nous.

    _____

3. —Voilà une pâtisserie. J'entre?
      —Oui, tu peux acheter des tartes.

    _____

4. —La petite Émilie monte?
      —Oui, elle doit faire sa sieste.

    _____

5. —Nous descendons?
      —Oui, vous pouvez faire les courses.

    _____

6. —Tu sors?
      —Oui, je veux retrouver mes copains.

    _____

7. —Vous rentrez?
      —Oui, nous voulons dîner.

    _____

8. —Corinne vient?
      —Oui, elle aime parler avec toi.

    _____

V. *Venir; Venir de + Infinitive*

VENIR *(TO COME)*

je viens	nous venons
tu viens	vous venez
il/elle/on vient	ils/elles viennent

■ When **venir** is followed directly by an infinitive it means *to come for the purpose of doing something*. When **venir** is followed by **de** + infinitive, it means *to have just done something*:

—Robert vient?	*Is Robert coming?*
—Oui. Il **vient** travailler avec toi.	*Yes, he's **coming** to work with you.*
—Vous **venez de** faire les courses?	***Have** you **just gone** shopping?*
—Oui. Je **viens d'**acheter du pain.	*Yes. I've **just bought** bread.*

K. C'est fait! Your friend asks if the people indicated have done certain things. Answer your friend in each case that the people have just done them.

Modèle   —Serge prépare le café?
    —Il vient de préparer le café.

1. —Monique sort?

    — _____

2. —Tu fermes les fenêtres?

    — _____

3. —Luc et Sylvie font les courses?

    — _____

4. —Marc lave la voiture?

    — _____

5. —Je téléphone à Michelle?

    — _____

6. —Nous regardons une émission à la télé?

    — _____

7. —Les enfants font une sieste?

    — _____

8. —Ta mère rentre?

    — _____

L. **Questions personnelles.** Answer the following questions in complete French sentences.

1. Qu'est-ce que vous allez faire ce week-end, vous et vos amis?

   _____

2. Où est-ce tu veux passer l'été?

   _____

3. Qu'est-ce que tu dois faire ce soir?

   _____

4. Est-ce qu'on peut bien manger à la cantine de ton école?

   _____

5. À quelle heure est-ce que tu rentres manger ce soir?

   _____

6. Est-ce que tu peux toujours finir tes devoirs?

   _____

M. **Composition.** Make a list of four things that you (or a friend or you and your friends) want to do and of four things that you must do. Then combine them, telling why you can't do what you want to do and when you are going to do those things. Combine all the information into a paragraph.

Modèle   Mes amies Christine et Jacqueline **veulent** aller au cinéma, mais elles ne **peuvent** pas parce qu'elles **doivent** faire leurs devoirs. Elles **vont** aller au cinéma samedi soir.

Irregular Verbs: *prendre, mettre, lire, écrire, croire, voir, dire, rire, suivre, recevoir*

I. *Prendre*

- The verb **prendre** is irregular. Note that it has a double **n** in the third-person plural.

PRENDRE *(TO TAKE)*

je prends	nous prenons
tu prends	vous prenez
il/elle/on prend	ils/elles pre**nn**ent

The verb **prendre,** not **avoir,** is used to mean *to have* with items of food and drink.

—Je **prends** une glace. Et vous?   *I'm **having** ice cream. What about you?*

—Nous, nous **prenons** du yaourt.   *We're **having** yogurt.*

- The verbs **apprendre** *(to learn)* and **comprendre** *(to understand)* are conjugated like **prendre.**

APPRENDRE *(TO LEARN)*

je apprends	nous apprenons
tu apprends	vous apprenez
il/elle/on apprend	ils/elles appre**nn**ent

COMPRENDRE *(TO UNDERSTAND)*

je comprends	nous comprenons
tu comprends	vous comprenez
il/elle/on comprend	ils/elles compre**nn**ent

- Expressions with **prendre:**

  prendre des billets *to buy tickets*

  prendre le petit déjeuner *to have breakfast*

  prendre un café *to have a cup of coffee*

  prendre une décision *to make a decision*

A. On va à l'école. Use the verb **prendre** to tell what each of these people is taking to school.

Modèle Béatrice/son stylo
➤ Béatrice prend son stylo.

1. Sophie et Jeanne/leurs livres

   _____

2. Philippe/son cahier

   _____

3. Éric et moi/nos sacs à dos

   _____

4. toi/tes devoirs

   _____

5. vous/vos disquettes

   _____

6. Florence/ses crayons

   _____

7. moi/ma calculatrice

   _____

8. Aurélie/ses cassettes

   _____

B. À la cantine. What are people having for lunch today in the school cafeteria? Use the verb **prendre** to find out.

Modèle Luc/une pizza
➤ Luc prend une pizza.

1. moi/un sandwich au fromage

   _____

2. Cécile et Marc/des œufs

   _____

➤➤➤➤➤

3. vous/un yaourt

_____

4. nous/des spaghettis

_____

5. Frédéric/de la viande

_____

6. toi/une salade

_____

7. Isabelle/de la soupe

_____

8. on/un dessert

_____

C. On se prépare pour l'économie globale. All the people indicated can already understand one foreign language and have begun to learn a new one. Say so using the verbs **apprendre** and **comprendre**.

Modèle Jacques/japonais/chinois ➢
—Jacques apprend le japonais?
—Non. Il comprend déjà le japonais. Il apprend le chinois.

1. Nathalie/espagnol/portugais

— _____

— _____

2. Vincent et Joseph/allemand/russe

— _____

— _____

3. tu/français/italien

— _____

— _____

4. vous/anglais/français

   — _____

   — _____

5. Suzanne et Martine/russe/polonais

   — _____

   — _____

6. tu/grec/hébreu

   — _____

   — _____

7. Charles/arabe/turc

   — _____

   — _____

II. *Mettre*

■ **Mettre** is conjugated very much like an **-re** verb, but it has only one **t** in the singular.

METTRE *(TO PUT, TO PUT ON)*

je me**t**s	nous mettons
tu me**t**s	vous mettez
il/elle/on me**t**	ils/elles mettent

Mettre is used to mean *to put on* an article of clothing.

—Qu'est-ce que tu **mets** aujourd'hui? *What are you **putting on** (wearing) today?*

—Je **mets** ma nouvelle robe. *I'm **putting on** my new dress.*

■ Expressions with **mettre**:

mettre la table *to set the table*

mettre la télé, la radio, l'air conditionné *to turn on the TV, the radio, the air conditioner*

Je ne sais pas quoi mettre. *I don't know what to wear.*

D. Qu'est-ce qu'on met? Create dialogs about clothing using the verb **mettre.**

Modèle Jean/son bonnet/sa casquette ➤
  —Est-ce que Jean **met** son bonnet?
  —Non, il ne **met** pas son bonnet. Il **met** sa casquette.

Les vêtements

l'anorak *(masc.) ski jacket*   la chaussure *shoe*

le bas *stocking*   le chemisier *blouse*

le bonnet *woolen cap*   l'imperméable *(masc.) rain coat*

la botte *boot*   la jupe *skirt*

la casquette *helmet*   le pull *sweater*

la chaussette *sock*   le tee-shirt *T-shirt*

---

1. Monique/son chemisier/son pull

    — _____

    — _____

2. toi/ces chaussures/ces bottes

    — _____

    — _____

3. vous/ce pantalon/ces jupes

    — _____

    — _____

4. Albert/son tee-shirt/sa chemise blanche

    — _____

    — _____

5. les professeurs/leurs anoraks/leurs imperméables

— _____

— _____

6. toi/tes (mes) chaussettes/mes bas

— _____

— _____

III. *Lire* and *écrire*

LIRE *(TO READ)*

je lis	nous lisons
tu lis	vous lisez
il/elle/on lit	ils/elles lisent

ÉCRIRE *(TO WRITE)*

j'écris	nous écrivons
tu écris	vous écrivez
il/elle/on écrit	ils/elles écrivent

E. Qu'est-ce qu'ils font? Continue each of these sentences telling whether the people indicated are reading or writing.

Modèle Marie a un livre. ➤ Elle lit.

1. Jacques et Pierre ont un journal. _____

2. J'ai un crayon. _____

3. Tu as un stylo. _____

4. Ariane a un roman. _____

5. Nous avons des feutres. _____

6. Vous avez un article. _____

7. Nous avons des albums. _____

8. Vous avez un morceau de craie. _____

F. Conversation. Compose exchanges about reading and writing. The first speaker asks a question. The second answers it in the negative and points out that the person asked about is doing the other activity.

Modèle   Luc/lire ➤
              —Est-ce que Luc lit?
              —Non, il ne lit pas. Il écrit.

1. Odile et Laure/écrire

   — _____

   — _____

2. tu/écrire

   — _____

   — _____

3. vous/lire

   — _____

   — _____

4. Mariane/écrire

   — _____

   — _____

5. vous/écrire

   — _____

   — _____

6. tu/lire

   — _____

   — _____

7. les élèves/lire

   — _____

   — _____

IV. *Croire* and *voir*

- The verbs **croire** and **voir** have similar conjugations in the present tense.

CROIRE *(TO BELIEVE)*

je crois	nous croyons
tu crois	vous croyez
il/elle/on croit	ils/elles croient

VOIR *(TO SEE)*

je vois	nous voyons
tu vois	vous voyez
il/elle/on voit	ils/elles voient

- Expressions with **croire**:

  Je **crois** que oui. *I think so.*

  Je **crois** que non. *I don't think so.*

  Both **croire** and **voir** can be followed by dependent clauses beginning with **que**. The conjunction **que** is never left out in French as the conjunction *that* often is in English.

  Il croit **qu'**elle s'appelle Lisette.　　*He thinks (that) her name is Lisette.*

  Je vois **que** vous avez froid.　　*I see (that) you're cold.*

G. On se trompe. Use the verb **croire** + a dependent clause beginning with **que** to express the mistaken ideas some of these students have about other people. Use stressed pronouns where the subject is a pronoun.

Modèle　Joseph ne parle pas anglais./Marie
　　　➤ Mais Marie croit qu'il parle anglais.

1. Les Durand ne sont pas en vacances./leurs voisins

   _____

2. Laurent ne prend pas les billets./nous

   _____

3. Les étudiants ne sont pas en retard./le professeur

   _____

4. Solange ne comprend pas./toi

   _____

5. Elle ne sort pas avec Alain./moi

   _____

6. Maurice ne travaille pas ici./vous

_____

7. Chantal n'a pas beaucoup de disques compacts./tout le monde

_____

8. Paul n'est pas canadien./Albert et Jeanne

_____

H. Qui voit-on? Use the verb **voir** to tell whom the people indicated are seeing today. Use stressed pronouns where the subject is a pronoun.

Modèle   Michel/Anne ➢ Michel voit Anne.

1. nous/les copains

_____

2. toi/tes grands-parents

_____

3. Philippe/son oncle

_____

4. Nicole et Monique/leurs petits amis

_____

5. Olivier/ses cousins

_____

6. vous/vos professeurs

_____

7. moi/mon ami Victor

_____

8. mes parents/leurs voisins

_____

V. *Dire*

■ Notice the irregular **vous** form of the verb **dire**.

DIRE *(TO SAY, TO TELL)*

je dis	nous disons
tu dis	vous **dites**
il/elle/on dit	ils/elles disent

I. On ne dit rien. Construct a dialog asking what each person is saying and answering that each is not saying anything. Use the verb **dire** and the negative expression **ne... rien.**

Modèle   Marie-France ➤
—Qu'est-ce que Marie-France dit?
—Rien. Elle ne dit rien.

1. Chantal et Sabine

    — _____

    — _____

2. tu

    — _____

    — _____

3. vous *(pl.)*

    — _____

    — _____

4. Guillaume

    — _____

    — _____

5. nous

    — _____

    — _____

6. je

    — _____

    — _____

VI. *Rire, suivre,* and *recevoir*

RIRE *(TO LAUGH)*

je ris	nous rions
tu ris	vous riez
il/elle/on rit	ils/elles rient

SUIVRE *(TO FOLLOW)*

je suis	nous suivons
tu suis	vous suivez
il/elle/on suit	ils/elles suivent

Note that **je suis** can mean either *I follow* or *I am.* Context clarifies which is meant.

RECEVOIR *(TO RECEIVE, TO GET; TO HAVE COMPANY)*

je reçois	nous recevons
tu reçois	vous recevez
il/elle/on reçoit	ils/elles reçoivent

Note the use of the cedilla under the **c (ç)** in the singular and the **ils/elles** forms.

■ Expressions with **rire, suivre,** and **recevoir:**

recevoir son bulletin de notes *to get one's report card*

dire quelque chose pour rire *to say something as a joke*

à suivre *to be continued*

suivre un cours *to take a course*

suivre un régime *to be on a diet*

J. Les études. Tell what courses these people are taking to prepare for their chosen profession. Use the verbs **vouloir** and **suivre.** Follow the model.

Modèle   Jean/médecin/biologie
  ➤ Jean veut être médecin. Il suit des cours de biologie.

1. toi/interprète/japonais

   _____

2. Lise/femme d'affaires/gestion

   _____

3. vous/artiste/peinture

   _____

4. Charles et Marc/athlètes/culture physique

   _____

5. moi/professeur de littérature/français

_____

6. mon frère/programmeur/informatique

_____

7. nous/ingénieurs/maths

_____

8. mes sœurs/journalistes/histoire

_____

K. La communication moderne. Tell what kind of communication each of these people receives using the verb **recevoir.**

Modèle Yvette/une lettre ➤ Yvette reçoit une lettre.

La communication

la carte postale *postcard*

le colis *package*

le coup de téléphone *telephone call*

le courrier électronique *e-mail*

le faire-part *announcement* *(wedding, birth, etc.)*

le message *message*

la télécopie *fax*

---

1. nous/des télécopies

_____

2. vous/du courrier électronique

_____

3. mes parents/des cartes postales

_____

4. notre bureau/des colis

_____

5. Aurélie/un faire-part

_____

➤➤➤➤➤

6. moi/un coup de téléphone

_____

7. toi/un message

_____

Les industries de pointe (high tech)

France is well known abroad for its food and wine industries. It is not as widely known that France has also made important contributions in scientific and medical research and in the area of high technology during the past four decades.

- The **Pasteur** Institute near Paris was the first in the world to isolate the AIDS virus.
- The French space program has produced the **Ariane** satellite. Ariane satellites are launched from Kourou in French Guyana, South America.
- France leads the world in research in nuclear physics. The laboratories of **CERN, Centre Européan de Recherches nucléaires** is located near the Swiss border, and the **GANIL, Grand Accélérateur national d'ions lourds,** is located near the city of Caen in Normandy. Seventy-five percent of the electricity used in France is produced by nuclear plants.
- French scientists have discovered a new way to transfer data—such as text, voice, and images—at very high speeds: ATM (asynchronous transfer mode). ATM promises to play an important role in the creation of the electronic superhighway.

L. Comme c'est drôle. When these people read something funny (= **quelque chose de drôle**), they laugh. Say so using the verbs **lire** and **rire.**

Modèle Stéphane ➤ Quand Stéphane lit quelque chose de drôle, il rit.

1. tu

_____

2. nous

_____

3. ma petite sœur

_____

4. mes copines

_____

5. je

_____

6. vous

_____

M. Questions personnelles. Answer the following questions in complete French sentences.

1. Combien de cours suivez-vous cette année?

_____

2. Qu'est-ce que vous lisez en été? Des romans, des magazines, des essais?

_____

3. Est-ce que vous écrivez des lettres ou des messages électroniques?

_____

4. Qu'est-ce que vous recevez pour votre anniversaire?

_____

5. Qu'est-ce que vous prenez d'habitude pour le petit déjeuner?

_____

N. Composition. Write a connected paragraph of seven or eight sentences about your school. Talk about courses, what you learn, if you understand your teachers, what you read and write, etc.

*Gender and Number of Nouns; Definite, Indefinite, and Partitive Articles; **C'est** versus **il est***

I. Gender and Number of Nouns; the Definite and Indefinite Articles

French nouns are divided into two categories called genders. In French, the forms of the articles are different for masculine and feminine nouns.

■ The definite article corresponds to English *the*.

	masculine	feminine
singular	**le** magasin	**la** voiture
plural	**les** magasins	**les** voitures

The articles **le** and **la** change to **l'** before nouns beginning with a vowel or a mute **h**: **l'appartement** *(masc.) apartment*, **l'hôtel** *(masc.) hotel*, **l'école** *(fem.) school*, **l'heure** *(fem.) time, hour*.

■ The indefinite article corresponds to English *a, an*.

	masculine	feminine
singular	**un** magasin	**une** voiture
plural	**des** magasins	**des** voitures

Notes:

1. There is no English equivalent for the plural indefinite article **des**.

   Il vend **des** voitures américaines.   *He sells American cars.*

2. Most French nouns are made plural by adding **-s**. This **-s** is not pronounced.

   des ville**s**, les ami**s**

3. The indefinite articles **un, une, des** change to **de (d')** in negative sentences.

   —Tu as une voiture?   *Do you have a car?*
   —Non, je n'ai pas **de** voiture.   *No, I don't have a car.*

   The change of **un, une, des** to **de** does not take place if the verb is **être**.

   —C'est un chemisier, ça?   *Is that a blouse?*
   —Non, ce n'est pas **un** chemisier.   *No, it's not a blouse. It's a dress.*
     C'est une robe.

A. **Visite de la ville.** Gisèle is showing a friend around her city. Her friend asks if the city has certain places of interest. Gisèle points them out to her. Write their conversation. Notice in the model the difference in meaning between **il y a,** which indicates whether something exists, and **voilà,** which points something out. Use the definite and indefinite articles according to the model.

Modèle   jardin public ➤
         —Est-ce qu'il y a un jardin public?
         —Oui. Voilà le jardin public.

La ville

la cathédrale *cathedral*	**le parc** *park*
la gare *railway station*	**la place centrale** *town square*
l'hôtel *(masc.) hotel*	**le stade** *stadium*
le jardin public *public garden*	**le théâtre** *theatre*

---

1. stade

   — _____

   — _____

2. hôtels

   — _____

   — _____

3. cathédrale

   — _____

   — _____

4. parc

   — _____

   — _____

5. bibliothèque

   — _____

   — _____

➤➤➤➤➤

6. place centrale

——

——

7. théâtres

——

——

8. gare

——

——

La ville

French cities are different from American cities in a number of ways:

■ The railway station, **la gare,** is a place known to all inhabitants, and is evidence of the importance of rail travel in France. All cities and most towns are connected by train.

■ Many older cities preserve part or all of the medieval town they developed from. It forms the core of the city, around the cathedral and the main square.

■ Public transportation is much more common in France than in most American cities. In Paris there are two systems of urban rail transportation—the **métro,** or Paris subway system, and the **RER** (**Réseau Express Régional**) which links numerous suburbs of Paris to the city proper and to the **métro.**

■ Many government offices have no equivalents in the United States. The **Maison des Jeunes et de la Culture** is a network of community centers for young people found all over France. They offer sports and cultural facilities, and often sponsor theater, music, and dance performances. The **Syndicat d'initiative** is the tourist office. It offers maps and brochures about many facets of France that could be interesting to a visitor.

II. Gender of Nouns

The gender of a noun has to be memorized along with its meaning. Here are
a few guidelines to help you remember the gender of nouns, however.

■ Nouns referring to males are usually masculine; nouns referring to females
are feminine.

un frère	*a brother*	**une** sœur	*a sister*
un garçon	*a boy*	**une** fille	*a girl; a daughter*
un homme	*a man*	**une** femme	*a woman, a wife*
un taureau	*a bull*	**une** vache	*a cow*

■ Many nouns referring to males form corresponding nouns referring to
females by adding -**e.**

un ami ➤ une ami**e** *friend*

un avocat ➤ une avocat**e** *lawyer*

un cousin ➤ une cousin**e** *cousin*

■ Many nouns referring to males form their corresponding feminine forms
with feminine endings similar to those of adjectives.

ien ➤ ienne	un pharmac**ien**, une pharmac**ienne** *pharmacist* un Canad**ien**, une Canad**ienne** *Canadian*
on ➤ onne	un champ**ion**, une champ**ionne** *champion* un patr**on**, une patr**onne** *boss*
eur ➤ euse	un dans**eur**, une dans**euse** *dancer* un programm**eur**, une programm**euse** *programmer*
teur ➤ trice	un consomma**teur**, une consomma**trice** *consumer* un direc**teur**, une direc**trice** *manager*
er ➤ ère	un étrang**er**, une étrang**ère** *foreigner* un boulang**er**, une boulang**ère** *baker*
ier ➤ ière	un infirm**ier**, une infirm**ière** *nurse* un épic**ier**, une épic**ière** *grocer*

■ Some nouns referring to people (including nouns with the suffix -**iste**)
change the article rather than the ending to show whether a man or a
woman is referred to. The noun itself does not change.

un artiste, **une** artiste	**un** élève, **une** élève
un camarade, **une** camarade	**un** enfant, **une** enfant
un collègue, **une** collègue	**un** secrétaire, **une** secrétaire
un dentiste, **une** dentiste	

- The following nouns are always grammatically masculine even when they refer to women.[1]

un architecte *architect*   **un** médecin *doctor*

un auteur *author*   **un** peintre *painter*

un docteur *doctor*   **un** professeur *teacher*[2]

un écrivain *writer*   **un** sculpteur *sculptor*

Sa femme est un écrivain très connu.   *His wife is a very famous writer.*

Mon professeur s'appelle Marie Jobert.   *My teacher's name is Marie Jobert.*

- The following nouns are always grammatically feminine even if they refer to men.

une connaissance *acquaintance*   **une** vedette *film star*

une personne *person*   **une** victime *victim*

Son père est **une** des **victimes** de l'accident.   *His (Her) father is one of the victims of the accident.*

Marc est **une** bonne **personne**.   *Marc is a good person.*

B. Les gens. Complete the missing elements of the following list. Write the indefinite article with each noun.

masculine	feminine
1. un oncle	_____
2. _____	une mécanicienne
3. un sculpteur	_____
4. un socialiste	_____
5. _____	une victime
6. un auteur	_____
7. _____	une camarade
8. un enfant	_____
9. un boucher	_____
10. _____	une élève
11. un peintre	_____

---

[1]To specify reference to a woman, the phrases **une femme docteur, une femme auteur** are used.

[2]Colloquially, **la professeur** is sometimes used for a female teacher, especially among students.

12. _____   une journaliste

13. _____   une vendeuse

14. un employé   _____

15. un dessinateur   _____

16. _____   une voisine

17. un informaticien   _____

18. un réceptionniste   _____

III. More about Gender of Nouns

■ The following endings indicate that the noun is grammatically masculine.

-age	**un** avantage, **le** courage, **le** ménage *(housekeeping)*, **le** message, **un** orage *(storm)*, **un** sondage *(poll)*, **un** voyage (BUT: **la** page and **la** plage)
-eau	**le** bateau, **le** cadeau, **le** couteau, **le** gâteau, **le** niveau *(level)*, **le** rideau *(curtain)* (BUT: **l'**eau and **la** peau *(skin)* are feminine.)
-et	**le** carnet *(notebook)*, **l'**intérêt, **le** projet, **le** sujet
-ing	**le** camping, **le** pressing *(dry cleaner)*, **le** shampooing, **le** shopping
-ment	**le** commencement, **le** logement, **le** monument, **le** mouvement, **le** sentiment

■ The following endings indicate that the noun is grammatically feminine.

-ance	**une** ambiance, **la** chance, **la** distance, **l'**importance, **la** résistance, **la** séance *(showing)*
-ence	**une** apparence, **la** concurrence *(competition)*, **l'**essence *(gasoline)*, **une** expérience
-esse	**une** adresse, **la** jeunesse, **la** politesse, **la** promesse
-ette	**la** casquette, **la** cassette, **la** mobylette, **une** omelette, **la** raquette
-ière	**une** carrière, **la** cuisinière, **la** lumière, **la** manière
-ine	**une** aspirine, **la** discipline, **la** farine *(flour)*, **la** machine, **une** origine, **la** tartine (BUT: **le** magazine)
-sion	**la** décision, **une** expression, **la** permission
-té	**une** activité, **la** générosité, **la** publicité, **la** spécialité, **l'**université
-tion	**une** addition, **une** explication, **une** invitation, **la** natation *(swimming)*
-tude	**une** attitude, **une** habitude
-ure	**une** aventure, **la** couverture, **la** figure, **la** nourriture, **la** peinture, **la** voiture

- The ending -**on** (when it is not part of -**sion** or -**tion,** which indicate feminine nouns) appears on nouns of both genders.

masculine	feminine
l'avion *airplane*	la boisson *drink*
le balcon *balcony*	la chanson *song*
le crayon *pencil*	la comparaison *comparison*
le coton *cotton*	la façon *way, manner*
le jambon *ham*	la leçon *lesson*
le klaxon *car horn*	la maison *house*
le pantalon *pants*	la raison *reason*
le poisson *fish*	la saison *season*
le salon *living room*	
le savon *soap*	
le violon *violin*	

C. **Mon dictionnaire.** Complete this word list by adding the appropriate definite article and the definition. Select your definitions from the list.

belt	cheese	border	poll
station	truth	chalkboard	car
freedom	parking	napkin	store window
jam	acquaintance	front	scenery

1. _____ ceinture _____

2. _____ tableau _____

3. _____ fromage _____

4. _____ serviette _____

5. _____ vérité _____

6. _____ frontière _____

7. _____ stationnement _____

8. _____ paysage _____

9. _____ liberté _____

10. _____ connaissance _____

11. _____ sondage _____

12. _____ vitrine _____

D. Au pluriel. Indicate with a check mark whether the following nouns (which usually appear in the plural) are masculine or feminine, and write the English equivalent of each noun in the space provided.

noun	masc. plural	fem. plural	English
1. les lunettes	_____	_____	_____
2. les bagages	_____	_____	_____
3. les vacances	_____	_____	_____
4. les toilettes	_____	_____	_____
5. les médicaments	_____	_____	_____
6. les instructions	_____	_____	_____
7. les déchets	_____	_____	_____
8. les vêtements	_____	_____	_____

IV. Irregular Noun Plurals

Some nouns in French have irregular plurals.

■ Nouns ending in -s, -x, or -z in the singular do not add an -s in the plural.

le ta**s** *pile*	les tas
le pri**x** *price*	les prix
le ne**z** *nose*	les nez

■ Nouns ending in -**au**, -**eu** and some nouns ending in -**ou** form the plural by adding -**x,** not -**s.**

le bate**au** *boat*	les bateaux
le j**eu** *game*	les jeux
le gen**ou** *knee*	les genoux

Note, however: **les pneus** *(tires)*, **les clous** *(nails)*, **les trous** *(holes).*

■ Most nouns ending in -**al** change -**al** to -**aux** in the plural.

l'anim**al** *animal*	les anim**aux**
le génér**al** *general*	les génér**aux**

Note these exceptions: **les carnavals, les festivals.**

■ Some nouns have irregular plurals.

l'œil *eye*	**les yeux** *eyes*
le travail *work*	**les travaux** *projects, jobs, construction*
monsieur	**messieurs**
madame	**mesdames**
mademoiselle	**mesdemoiselles**

E. Au pluriel! Write the plural of the following phrases.

1. le cheval _____   7. le journal _____

2. un cours _____   8. le bureau _____

3. la voix _____   9. le mois _____

4. le clou _____   10. le cheveu _____

5. un trou _____   11. le festival _____

6. un bijou _____   12. l'œil _____

V. The Partitive Article

■ In addition to the definite and indefinite articles, French has a third article called the partitive article. The partitive is used before nouns that cannot be counted, such as meat, gold, water, air. Here are the forms of the partitive article.

masculine	feminine	nouns beginning with a vowel or a mute *h*
du pain *bread*	**de la** sauce *sauce*	**de l'**énergie *energy*
du bœuf *beef*	**de la** moutarde *mustard*	**de l'**essence *gasoline*

—Tu veux **du** thé?   *Do you want (**some**) tea?*
—Non, je veux **de l'**eau minérale.   *No, I want (**some**) mineral water.*

The partitive has the same form in the plural as the indefinite article: **des** œufs *(eggs)*, **des** légumes *(vegetables)*, **des** bonbons *(candy)*.

After a negative word the partitive article, like the indefinite article, becomes **de** (**d'** before a vowel or a mute **h**).

—Tu ne fais pas **d'**exercice?   *You're not doing **any** exercise?*
—Non, je n'ai pas **d'**énergie.   *No, I don't have **any** energy.*

- The partitive article also becomes **de (d')** after quantity words and expressions.

beaucoup de *much, many, a lot of*	**une bouteille de** *a bottle of*
peu de *little, few*	**un kilo de** *a kilogram of*
un peu de *a little*	**une boîte de** *a box of*
trop de *too much, too many*	**une livre de** *a pound of*
tant de *so much, so many*	**cent grammes de** *100 grams of*
autant de *as much, as many*	**une douzaine de** *a dozen*
assez de *enough*	**une tranche de** *a slice of*
combien de *how much, how many*	**un tas de** *a heap of, a whole lot of*
moins de *fewer, less*	**pas mal de** *a lot of (colloquial)*
plus de *no more, more*	**énormément de** *an awful lot of*

- In everyday French, **encore** + the partitive is used to mean *more*. The partitive is not reduced to **de. Plus de** after a negative means *no more*.

—Encore **de la** viande?	*(Would you like)* **some** *more meat?*
—Merci, je ne veux **plus de** viande.	*No thank you, I don't want* **any** *more meat.*

- The full partitive (**de** + article) is used after **la plupart** *(most, the majority of)*.

La plupart des étudiants arrivent à l'heure.	*The majority of students arrive on time.*

The phrase **ne... que** *(only)* is not a negative, and the partitive is not reduced to **de** before a noun that follows it.

—Lui, il **ne** boit **que** de l'eau.	*He drinks only water.*
—Et toi, tu **ne** bois **que** du thé.	*And you drink only tea.*

- Note the use of the partitive with the verb **faire** to refer to school subjects and sports.

faire **de la** chimie	*to study, take, major in chemistry*
faire **du** ski	*to go skiing, do skiing as a sport*

- The partitive is reduced to **de** when an adjective precedes the noun.

—J'ai acheté **de** bonnes tartes pour ce soir.	*I have bought good pastries for this evening.*
—Et moi, j'ai acheté **de** belles fleurs.	*And I have bought beautiful flowers.*

However, this rule is often disregarded in both speech and writing: **des** bonnes tartes, **des** belles fleurs.

F. **Les courses.** Add the correct forms of the partitive article to these conversations about food shopping.

—Tu descends avec moi? On n'a pas _____ (1) viande pour le dîner.

—Tu vas acheter _____ (2) viande? Moi, je voudrais _____ (3) poisson.

—C'est une bonne idée. On doit aussi prendre _____ (4) légumes.

—Lesquels? _____ (5) carottes et _____ (6) pommes de terre?

—Pourquoi pas? Et _____ (7) salade aussi.

—N'oublie pas d'acheter _____ (8) eau minérale.

—Demain nous recevons _____ (9) amis américains pour le petit déjeuner.

—Qu'est-ce que vous allez servir?

—Bon, nous avons _____ (10) café et _____ (11) thé. On va acheter _____ (12) pain.

—Vous n'achetez _____ (13) œufs? Je crois que les Américains mangent _____ (14) œufs le matin.

—Non, je ne crois pas. Nous, on ne mange pas _____ (15) œufs pour le petit déjeuner. Je crois que je vais acheter beaucoup _____ (16) croissants et _____ (17) confiture.

G. **Au garde-manger.** *(In the pantry.)* Mme Gaudry is checking over her stock of food. Add the words in parentheses to each of the sentences to find out what she has and what she's running out of.

Modèle   J'ai de la limonade. *(trois bouteilles)*
➤ J'ai trois bouteilles de limonade.

1. Il y a des céréales. *(beaucoup)*

    _____

2. Nous avons du pain. *(peu)*

    _____

3. J'ai acheté des chocolats. *(une boîte)*

    _____

4. Je vois du café. *(un kilo)*

   _____

5. Il y a du thon. *(un tas)*

   _____

6. J'ai des spaghettis. *(tant)*

   _____

7. Il y a du fromage. *(deux cents grammes)*

   _____

8. Il y a aussi des œufs. *(une douzaine)*

   _____

VI. Some Special Uses of the Articles

■ The definite article in French, as in English, is used to refer to specific items, things that are known to both the person talking and the person spoken to.

—Où est **la** librairie?	*Where is the bookstore?*
—Là-bas, en face de **la** place.	*There, across from the square.*

■ Unlike English, French also requires the definite article before nouns used in a general sense. This use is especially common after verbs expressing likes and dislikes.

—Aimes-tu **l'**histoire?	*Do you like history?*
—Oui, mais je préfère **les** maths.	*Yes, but I prefer math.*

This use of the definite article is common with nouns that refer to abstract ideas.

Nous sommes pour **la** liberté et **la** tolérance.	*We are for freedom and tolerance.*
La bonté et **la** générosité sont des qualités importantes.	*Kindness and generosity are important traits.*

■ With foods, the articles convey different meanings. The definite article is used to refer to dishes on a menu.

—Pour vous, monsieur?	*What will you have, sir?*
—**L'**agneau.	*Lamb* (= the lamb dish on the menu).
—Et pour madame?	*And what will you have, madam?*
—Pour moi, **le** coq au vin.	*Chicken in wine sauce.*

- The indefinite article indicates a usual serving (especially in a restaurant).

  un café   *a cup of coffee*

  une limonade   *a glass of lemonade*

- The partitive article indicates an indefinite quantity.

  —Tu veux boire **de l'**eau minérale?   *Do you want to have (some) mineral*
                                                water?

  —Non, merci. Tu as **du** thé?   *No, thanks. Do you have (any) tea?*

- Study the uses of the articles with the word **café** in the following sentences.

  Le café est cultivé au Brésil.   *Coffee is grown in Brazil.*
                                                (general sense)

  Je n'aime pas **le** café qu'elle prépare.   *I don't like her coffee (the coffee she*
                                                makes). (specific)

  Un café, s'il vous plaît.   *A cup of coffee, please.*
                                                (standard serving)

  Le matin je prends **du** café.   *In the morning I have coffee.*
                                                (indefinite quantity)

H. Complete the following conversations with the missing articles.

Au café

LOUIS   Garçon! _____ (1) café pour moi et _____ (2) jus de
          pommes pour mademoiselle, s'il vous plaît!

GARÇON   Je suis désolé, monsieur, mais nous n'avons pas _____ (3) jus
          de pommes.

YVETTE   Bon, _____ (4) citron pressé, alors.

LOUIS   Garçon, _____ (5) addition, s'il vous plaît.

GARÇON   Voilà _____ (6) addition, monsieur.

LOUIS   Est-ce que _____ (7) service est compris?

GARÇON   Oui, monsieur.

Un lycée moderne

MONIQUE   Est-ce que vous avez _____ (8) ordinateurs dans votre lycée,
          Béatrice?

BÉATRICE Oui, _____ (9) ordinateurs sont très importants dans notre
          lycée.

MONIQUE   Est-ce que tu fais _____ (10) informatique?

BÉATRICE Maintenant je ne fais pas _____ (11) informatique, mais l'année
          prochaine je vais suivre un cours pour apprendre à programmer.

MONIQUE   As-tu _____ (12) ordinateur à la maison?

BÉATRICE   Oui, la plupart _____ (13) étudiants ont un ordinateur chez

eux. Nous avons _____ (14) nouveaux ordinateurs avec

beaucoup de mémoire.

VII. *Il/elle est* versus *c'est* + Noun

There are two ways to identify a person in French, that is, to express *he's a, she's a.*

- **Il est/elle est** is used before a noun denoting profession, religion or nationality when there is no adjective. Unlike English, French requires no article in this construction.

—Elle est avocate?	*Is she a lawyer?*
—Non, son mari est avocat. Elle, elle est médecin.	*No, her husband is a lawyer. She's a doctor.*
—Les Smith sont Américains?	*Are the Smiths Americans?*
—Lui, il est Américain. Elle, elle est Anglaise.	*He's an American. She's an Englishwoman.*

- Before an adjective or an article, **c'est** must be used.

C'est un scientifique?	*Is he a scientist?*
Oui, c'est un scientifique très connu.	*Yes, he's a very famous scientist.*

I. Encore plus précis. Rewrite the following sentences adding the word(s) in parentheses.

Modèle   Elle est vendeuse. *(nouvelle)* ➤ C'est une nouvelle vendeuse.

1. Il est catholique. *(français)*

   _____

2. Elles sont programmeuses. *(nouvelles)*

   _____

3. Elle est artiste. *(connue)*

   _____

4. Il est informaticien. *(bon)*

   _____

5. Ils sont médecins. *(vieux, étrangers)*

   _____

➤➤➤➤➤

6. Il est soldat. *(canadien)*

_____

7. Elle est pharmacienne. *(patiente)*

_____

J. Questions personnelles. Answer these questions in complete French sentences.

1. Qu'est-ce que vous prenez pour le petit déjeuner?

_____

2. Combien de livres lisez-vous par an? Beaucoup? Peu? Trop?

_____

3. Qu'est-ce que vous préférez—la viande, le poulet ou le poisson?

_____

4. Quels desserts aimez-vous?

_____

5. Quelles qualités sont importantes dans un(e) ami(e)?

_____

K. Composition. Write a paragraph of seven to ten sentences talking about what you and your friends like to do: the sports you play, the music you listen to, the foods you eat, and the things that are important to you.

Adjectives: Forms, Position, Comparative, Superlative

I. Regular Adjectives

■ Adjectives in French agree in gender and number with the nouns they modify. Most adjectives add **-e** to form the feminine and **-s** to form the plural.

	masculine	feminine
singular	fort	forte
plural	forts	fortes

	masculine	feminine
singular	noir	noire
plural	noirs	noires

	masculine	feminine
singular	fatigué	fatiguée
plural	fatigués	fatiguées

	masculine	feminine
singular	joli	jolie
plural	jolis	jolies

■ Adjectives ending in mute **-e** do not add another **-e** for the feminine. They add **-s** to form the plural, but have the same form for both genders.

	masculine & feminine
singular	difficile
plural	difficiles

A. Aussi. Tell your friend the second person or thing she asks about has the same characteristic as the first one she mentions.

Modèle   —Lucille est petite. Et son frère?
➤ —Il est petit aussi.

1. —Odile est charmante. Et son petit ami?

   —_____

2. —Philippe est poli. Et ses sœurs?

   —_____

3. —Ce projet est compliqué. Et cette histoire?

   —_____

➤➤➤➤➤

4. —Cette place est agréable. Et le jardin?

   — _____

5. —Le tableau est joli. Et les dessins?

   — _____

6. —Ton sac est lourd. Et tes valises?

   — _____

7. —Luc est brun. Et ses cousines?

   — _____

II. Irregular Adjectives

Many French adjectives are irregular in their formation of the feminine or the plural or both.

■ Adjectives ending in -**x** or -**s** do not add an additional -**s** in the masculine plural.

un garçon chanceu**x** _a lucky boy_ ➤ des garçons chanceu**x**

un livre épai**s** _a thick book_ ➤ des livres épai**s**

■ Most adjectives ending in -**x** form the feminine by changing the -**x** to -**se.**

	masculine	feminine
singular	heureux	heureuse
plural	heureux	heureuses

	masculine	feminine
singular	merveilleux	merveilleuse
plural	merveilleux	merveilleuses

Exceptions: some one-syllable adjectives ending in -**x** have different formations in the feminine. Study the forms of **doux** (_sweet, gentle, soft_), **faux** (_false_), and **roux** (_redheaded, ruddy_).

	masculine	feminine
singular	doux	douce
plural	doux	douces

	masculine	feminine
singular	faux	fausse
plural	faux	fausses

	masculine	feminine
singular	roux	rousse
plural	roux	rousses

■ Most adjectives ending in -s, such as **gris** *(gray)*, **exquis** *(exquisite)* form the feminine regularly by adding -e (**grise, exquise**). A few, like **gros** *(big, fat)* and **gras** *(fat, fatty)*, form the feminine by adding -se.

	masculine	feminine
singular	gros	grosse
plural	gros	grosses

The adjectives **épais** *(thick)* and **bas** *(low)* also double the final -s before adding the -e of the feminine: (**épaisse, basse**).

■ Adjectives that end in -f in the masculine singular change -f to -ve in the feminine.

	masculine	feminine
singular	actif	active
plural	actifs	actives

■ Adjectives ending in -er in the masculine singular, such as **léger** *(light, not heavy)* change the -er to -ère to form the feminine.

	masculine	feminine
singular	léger	légère
plural	légers	légères

■ Adjectives ending in -el, -en, or -on in the masculine singular, such as **cruel** *(cruel)*, **italien** *(Italian)* and **bon** *(good)* double the final consonant before the feminine ending -e.

	masculine	feminine
singular	cruel	cruelle
plural	cruels	cruelles

	masculine	feminine
singular	italien	italienne
plural	italiens	italiennes

	masculine	feminine
singular	bon	bonne
plural	bons	bonnes

■ The adjectives **gentil** *(nice, friendly)* and **pareil** *(similar)* also double the final -l before adding -e to form the feminine.

	masculine	feminine
singular	gentil	gentille
plural	gentils	gentilles

	masculine	feminine
singular	pareil	pareille
plural	pareils	pareilles

■ Here are other adjectives with irregular feminine forms. The plurals are formed by adding -s.

masculine	feminine	masculine	feminine
blanc *white*	blan**che**	inquiet *worried, restless*	inqui**ète**
bref *brief*	br**ève**	long *long*	long**ue**
complet *complete*	compl**ète**	neuf *new*	neu**ve**
favori *favorite*	favor**ite**	public *public*	publi**que**
fou *crazy*	fo**lle**	sec *dry*	s**èche**
frais *fresh, cool*	fra**îche**	secret *secretive*	secr**ète**

■ The adjectives **chic** (*stylish*) and **marron** (*brown*) are invariable. They do not change form to reflect gender or number.

Il met des chaussures **marron**.   *He's putting on brown shoes.*

■ Some adjective plurals in French are irregular. The adjectives **beau** (*beautiful*) and **nouveau** (*new*) add -x to form the masculine plural: **beaux, nouveaux.** Most adjectives ending in -al have a masculine plural in -aux. The feminine plural is regular.

	masculine	feminine
singular	normal	normale
plural	norm**aux**	normales

The adjective **final** is an exception. Its masculine plural is **finals.**

B. Substitution. Rewrite each of these phrases substituting the noun in parentheses for the original noun.

Modèle   un nom étranger *(langues)* ➤ des langues étrangères

1. un monument ancien *(ville)*   _____

2. un roman passionnant *(histoires)*   _____

3. une glace délicieuse *(dessert)*   _____

4. une actrice connue *(acteur)*   _____

5. une famille allemande *(amis)*   _____

6. un chemin dangereux *(route)*   _____

7. un goût amer *(boisson)*   _____

8. des garçons sportifs *(filles)*   _____

9. une idée générale *(débats)*   _____

10. un homme roux *(femme)*   _____

11. une grosse voiture *(camion)*   _____

12. un long voyage *(conversation)* _____

13. un pantalon blanc *(chaussettes)* _____

14. du lait frais *(crème)* _____

C. À l'école. Create phrases that could be useful in talking about school by adding the correct forms of the adjectives given.

1. étranger

    a. une étudiante _____

    b. des revues _____

    c. des professeurs _____

2. final

    a. la classe _____

    b. les examens _____

    c. les rédactions _____

3. intéressant

    a. des cours _____

    b. des activités _____

    c. une lecture _____

4. sportif

    a. des étudiants _____

    b. des organisations _____

    c. une épreuve _____

D. Descriptions. Write a sentence describing each of these people and animals. Choose two adjectives for each and describe either what they look like or their personality.

Modèle   *(ton frère ou ta sœur)* ➤ Mon frère Samuel est grand et sympathique.

1. *(tes parents)*

    _____

2. *(ton frère ou ta sœur)*

    _____

➤➤➤➤➤

3. *(tes copains)*

_____

4. *(ton petit ami ou ta petite amie)*

_____

5. *(ton meilleur ami ou ta meilleure amie)*

_____

6. *(tes professeurs)*

_____

7. *(ton chien ou ton chat)*

_____

III. Position of Adjectives and Irregular Adjectives

■ Most French adjectives follow the noun they modify. In English, adjectives precede the noun.

C'est un livre **difficile.**	*It's a difficult book.*
Je suis des cours **intéressants.**	*I'm taking interesting courses.*

A few common French adjectives, such as those referring to beauty, age, goodness, and size, are usually placed before the noun.

beau *beautiful, handsome*	**joli** *pretty*
bon *good*	**long** *long*[1]
gentil *nice, friendly*	**mauvais** *bad*
grand *big*	**nouveau** *new*
gros *big, fat*	**petit** *small*
jeune *young*	**vieux** *old*

Ils ont une **grande** maison près d'un **joli** parc.	*They have a **big** house near a **pretty** park.*

The adjectives **beau, nouveau,** and **vieux** become **bel, nouvel,** and **vieil,** respectively, before masculine nouns beginning with a vowel or a mute **h.**

un **beau** jardin	un **nouveau** jardin	un **vieux** jardin
un **bel** arbre	un **nouvel** arbre	un **vieil** arbre

---

[1]**Long** often follows its noun in spoken French.

Here is a summary of the forms of these three adjectives:

	masculine	feminine
singular	beau/bel	belle
plural	beaux	belles

	masculine	feminine
singular	nouveau/nouvel	nouvelle
plural	nouveaux	nouvelles

	masculine	feminine
singular	vieux/vieil	vieille
plural	vieux	vieilles

Note that the same form is used in the masculine plural whether the following noun begins with a consonant or a vowel: de **beaux** anoraks, de **beaux** manteaux.

E. **Qui est-elle?** A mysterious woman has appeared in town. Describe her by adding the adjectives in parentheses to the sentences below.

Modèle Il y a une personne dans notre village. *(nouveau)*
➤ Il y a une nouvelle personne dans notre village.

1. C'est une femme. *(joli)*

   _____

2. Elle porte des lunettes. *(noir)*

   _____

3. Elle a des vêtements. *(exquis)*

   _____

4. Elle porte un chapeau. *(grand)*

   _____

5. C'est une personne. *(secret)*

   _____

6. Elle habite dans un hôtel. *(vieux)*

   _____

7. Elle parle une langue. *(étranger)*

   _____

8. C'est une femme. *(mystérieux)*

   _____

Les étrangers en France

Unlike some of her neighbors, such as Italy and Germany, France has never been a country of emigrants. A relatively small percentage of French people leave the country to make their lives abroad. However, France is a country of immigrants, who have been attracted by political freedom and economic opportunity. After World War II, France received millions of workers from Spain, Italy, and Portugal, many of whom chose to stay in the country. From the 1960s on, most immigrants to France have been from France's former colonies in North Africa: Tunisia, Algeria, and Morocco. Most French cities today have substantial Arabic-speaking communities, a network of mosques, and North African foodstores and restaurants.

IV. More on Position of Adjectives

■ Certain other adjectives always precede their nouns.

1. Ordinal numbers

   Nous habitons au **dixième** étage.   *We live on the eleventh floor.*

   Je descends au **troisième** arrêt.   *I get off at the third stop.*

2. These common adjectives

   autre *other*

   chaque *each*

   plusieurs *several*

   quelques *(pl.) a few*

   tel *(fem. **telle**) such a*

   Chaque salle de classe a **quelques** cassettes.   *Each classroom has **a few** cassettes.*

   Plusieurs étudiants lisent un autre livre.   ***Several** students are reading another book.*

■ Some adjectives have different meanings depending on whether they are placed before or after a noun.

mon **ancien** professeur	*my **former** teacher*
des traditions **anciennes**	***ancient** traditions*
ma **chère** amie	*my **dear** friend*
une bicyclette **chère**	*an **expensive** bicycle*
la **dernière** classe	*the **last** (final) class*
la semaine **dernière**	***last** week*
un **pauvre** homme	*a **poor** (**unfortunate**) man*
un homme **pauvre**	*a **poor** man (who has no money)*
ma **propre** chambre	*my **own** room*
une chambre **propre**	*a **clean** room*

une **sale** rue	a **nasty** (**awful**) street
une rue **sale**	a **dirty** street
le **seul** étudiant	the **only** student
un étudiant **seul**	a **lonely** student
un **vrai** problème	a **real** problem
une histoire **vraie**	a **true** story

F. Décrivez. Put the correct form of the adjective in parentheses either before or after the noun to create a logical sentence.

1. *(dernier)* C'est notre _____ classe _____! Les vacances commencent demain!

2. *(seul)*

   —Janine n'a pas d'amis.

   —Je sais. C'est une _____ fille _____.

3. *(sale)* Lise habite dans un _____ appartement

   _____ parce qu'elle ne le nettoie jamais.

4. *(cher)* Regarde le prix des dîners! C'est un _____ restaurant

   _____.

5. *(propre)* Je peux téléphoner quand je veux parce que j'ai mon

   _____ téléphone _____.

6. *(pauvre)*

   —Michel s'est cassé la jambe!

   —Le _____ garçon _____!

7. *(vrai)*

   —Je ne trouve pas mes lunettes. Où sont-elles?

   —C'est un _____ mystère _____.

G. Décrivons! Describe each of the nouns given by adding the adjective in parentheses. Pay attention to the agreement and position of the adjectives.

Modèle   avion *(grand)* ➤ un grand avion

1. ordinateur *(nouveau)*   _____

2. objet *(vieux)*   _____

3. idées *(mauvais)*   _____

4. ingénieur *(jeune)*   _____

➤➤➤➤➤

5. paquet *(gros)* _____

6. poire *(délicieux)* _____

7. endroits *(autre)* _____

8. baguettes *(croustillant)* _____

9. imprimante *(vieux)* _____

10. immeuble *(beau)* _____

11. île *(beau)* _____

12. forêt *(joli)* _____

13. église *(vieux)* _____

14. boîte *(petit)* _____

V. Comparison

■ French uses the following constructions to compare things or people.

plus + adjective + **que**	*more* + adjective + *than*
moins + adjective + **que**	*less* + adjective + *than*
aussi + adjective + **que**	*as* + adjective + *as*

La mobylette est **plus** rapide **que** la bicyclette.	*The moped is **faster** than the bicycle.*
Mais la mobylette est **moins** rapide **qu'**une voiture.	*But the moped is **less** fast than a car.*
La bicyclette est **aussi** rapide **que** le vélo tout terrain.	*The bicycle is **as** fast **as** the mountain bike.*

■ The usual English equivalent of a comparison with **moins** is *not as* + adjective + *as*:

L'école est **moins grande que** le lycée.	*The elementary school is **not as big as** the high school.*

■ The adjectives **bon** and **mauvais** have irregular comparative forms. They do not use the construction **plus** + adjective + **que.**

mauvais(e)(s) ➤ pire(s) *worse*

bon(ne)(s) ➤ meilleur(e)(s) *better*

Le livre est **meilleur que** le film.	*The book is **better** than the film.*
Ce restaurant est **pire que** l'autre.	*This restaurant is **worse** than the other.*

■ Note also the following forms.

mon frère **aîné,** ma sœur **aînée**   *my older brother, sister*

mon frère **cadet,** ma sœur **cadette**   *my younger brother, sister*

■ The stressed pronouns often appear after **que** in comparative sentences.

Mon frère est plus petit que **moi.**   *My brother is shorter than I am.*

Je suis moins sportif que **lui.**   *I'm less athletic than he is.*

Il est aussi impatient que **toi.**   *He is as impatient as you are.*

H. Notre lycée. Compare different aspects of this **lycée.**

Modèle   notre lycée/+ grand/l'école primaire
➤ Notre lycée est plus grand que l'école primaire.

1. le directeur/+ stricte/les professeurs

_____

2. nos devoirs/+ difficiles/les rédactions

_____

3. la cantine/− spacieuse/la salle de permanence

_____

4. les salles de classe/+ nombreuses/bureaux

_____

5. le laboratoire de chimie/= moderne/le laboratoire de biologie

_____

6. le lycée/− vaste/le terrain de sport

_____

7. la piscine/+ bonne/le gymnase

_____

8. les examens/+ mauvais/les devoirs

_____

I. **Résumé.** Summarize the information using a comparative construction.

Modèle Le pantalon coûte 500F. La jupe coûte 600F. ➤
(*chère*) La jupe <u>est plus chère que</u> le pantalon.

1. Jacques fait de la natation et du jogging. Marc joue aux échecs.

   (*sportif*) Jacques _____ Marc.

2. Paris a deux millions d'habitants. Lyon a 500,000 habitants.

   (*grand*) Lyon _____ Paris.

3. Monique attend le feu vert avant de traverser la rue. Christine traverse la rue sans regarder.

   (*prudente*) Christine _____ Monique.

4. Dans le cours d'histoire nous lisons 200 pages par semaine. Dans le cours d'anglais nous lisons 50 pages par semaine.

   (*difficile*) L'histoire _____ l'anglais.

5. Odile a dix ans. Justine a dix ans.

   (*jeune*) Odile _____ Justine.

6. Maurice pèse 60 kilos. Albert pèse 65 kilos.

   (*gros*) Maurice _____ Albert.

VI. The Superlative

The superlative of adjectives (English *most, least*) is formed using **plus** (*most*) or **moins** (*least*) according to the following patterns.

Adjective following noun

le/la/les + noun + **le/la/les** $\begin{Bmatrix} \textbf{plus} \\ \textbf{moins} \end{Bmatrix}$ + adjective + **de**

Montrez-moi **la** maison **la plus** élégante **de** la ville.	*Show me the most elegant house in the city.*

Adjective preceding noun

Montrez-moi **les plus** vielles maisons **du** village.	*Show me the oldest houses in the village.*

■ The preposition *in* after a superlative is **de**, not **dans**.

Philippe est le meilleur étudiant **de** la classe.	*Philippe is the best student in the class.*
C'est le journal le plus important **du** pays.	*It's the most important newspaper in the country.*

J. Mes copains. List your friends' outstanding characteristics. Create a superlative construction and make the adjective agree in gender and number with the person it refers to.

Modèle   Jean (+ grand) ➤ Jean est le plus grand.

1. Aurélie (+ intelligent)   _____

2. Serge et Marc (+ généreux)   _____

3. Claudine (− patient)   _____

4. Gisèle et Danielle (− sportif)   _____

5. Olivier (+ sociable)   _____

6. Luc (+ sérieux)   _____

7. Mireille (− travailleur)   _____

8. Solange et Paul (+ bavard)   _____

K. Liste touristique. Françoise has made a list of what she wants to see during her vacation. Write out her preferences as superlatives and make the adjectives agree.

Modèle   lac/beau/pays ➤ Le plus beau lac du pays

1. ville/grand/pays   _____

2. rues/animé/capitale   _____

3. musée/intéressant/ville   _____

4. église/vieux/région   _____

5. magasins/cher/ville   _____

6. restaurants/bon/pays   _____

L. Questions personnelles. Answer the following questions in complete French sentences, making sure to use adjectives in each case.

1. Quelle sorte de films aimez-vous voir?

   _____

2. Comment est votre quartier? Votre ville?

   _____

3. Décrivez votre école.

   _____

➤➤➤➤➤

4. Décrivez votre professeur idéal.

_____

5. Comment sont les émissions que vous regardez à la télé?

_____

M. Composition. Choose two of the following three topics and write a paragraph on each. Use as many adjectives as possible.

- ma maison idéale
- mon travail idéal
- mon mari idéal/ma femme idéale/mon ami(e) idéal(e)

Question Formation

I. *Yes/no* Questions

■ *Yes/no* questions expect the answers *yes* or *no*. There are three ways to form *yes/no* questions in French.

1. Keep the same word order as in statements, but add a question mark, which indicates that the voice rises at the end of the question. This pattern, called *intonation change,* is typical of colloquial language.

Tu travailles aujourd'hui?	*Are you working today?*
Madame Verdier est là?	*Is Mrs. Verdier in?*

2. Place the phrase **est-ce que** (**est-ce qu'**) at the beginning of a statement. **Est-ce que** can be used in all styles, both formal and informal.

Est-ce que tu travailles aujourd'hui?	*Are you working today?*
Est-ce qu'Anne est là?	*Is Anne in?*

3. Place the subject pronoun after the verb. The pronoun is attached to the subject with a hyphen. This pattern, called *inversion,* is typical of formal language.

Travailles-**tu** aujourd'hui?	*Are you working today?*

■ In inversion, if the subject is a noun, the corresponding pronoun is added after the verb, and the noun subject remains in its original position.

Madame Verdier est-**elle** là?	*Is Mrs. Verdier in?*
Les **étudiants** comprennent-**ils**?	*Do the students understand?*

■ When the pronouns **il, elle,** and **on** are placed after verb forms that end in a vowel, -**t**- is inserted between the verb and the pronoun.

Ce monsieur parle-**t**-il français?	*Does this gentleman speak French?*
Jeanne va-**t**-elle en France?	*Is Jeanne going to France?*
Y a-**t**-il un car pour Dijon?	*Is there a bus for Dijon?*
Dîne-**t**-on à six heures?	*Is dinner at six? Does one dine at six?*

■ In negative questions formed by means of inversion, **ne** and **pas** are placed around the inverted pronoun and verb.

N'explique-t-il **pas** bien?	*Doesn't he explain well?*
Ne savez-vous **pas** l'adresse?	*Don't you know the address?*

■ Note that the pronoun **je** is never inverted.

A. Un nouvel appartement. Carole is talking about an apartment with a real estate agent. Rephrase her questions using inversion.

Modèle   L'appartement a tous les conforts modernes?
> L'appartement a-t-il tous les conforts modernes?

Le logement

l'appartement *(masc.) apartment*   le loyer *rent*

l'ascenseur *(masc.) elevator*   modéré *moderate, reasonable*

donner sur *to face*   la pièce *room*

le logement *housing*   la salle à manger *dining room*

---

1. L'immeuble est près du métro?

   _____

2. Les pièces sont grandes?

   _____

3. Il y a une salle à manger?

   _____

4. Le loyer est modéré?

   _____

5. Les fenêtres donnent sur la rue?

   _____

6. La rue est tranquille?

   _____

7. L'ascenseur marche bien?

   _____

8. On peut visiter l'appartement?

   _____

Le TGV

The French high-speed train (**train à grande vitesse** or **TGV**) has revolutionized ground transportation in Europe. By 1999, the trip from Paris to Marseilles, a distance of 700 kilometers, will have been cut from eight to three hours. Most of France's major cities are linked by the high-speed rail network, and foreign cities such as Amsterdam, Frankfurt, Geneva, Rome, and Madrid are also connected. The high-speed trains run on special tracks and have an aerodynamic shape. The most modern ones reach speeds of 350 kilometers per hour.

B. Un voyage dans le train. A group of tourists is asking their guide questions about the train trip they are taking from Marseilles to Paris. Rephrase all their questions using inversion.

Modèle   Le train part à huit heures?
➤ Le train part-il à huit heures?

1. Nous prenons le TGV?

   _____

2. On sert le petit déjeuner dans le train?

   _____

3. Les places sont réservées?

   _____

4. Nous allons à la gare en taxi?

   _____

5. Vous allez avec nous?

   _____

6. Les porteurs vont mettre nos valises dans le train?

   _____

7. Le train arrive à Paris à une heure moins vingt?

   _____

8. Nous descendons dans un bon hôtel à Paris?

   _____

II. Question Words

■ To ask information questions, in which the expected answer is a piece of information, question words are commonly used in French.

Combien (de)? *How much?, How many?*	**Quand?** *When?*
Comment? *How?*	**Que?** *What?*
Où? *Where?* **D'où?** *Where from?*	**Quel(le)(s)?** *Which?*
Pourquoi? *Why?*	**Qui?** *Who? Whom?*

■ Questions using question words can be formed with intonation change, with **est-ce que,** or with inversion.

Tu vas où? ↗	*Where are you going?*
Pourquoi **sortez-vous?**	*Why are you leaving?*
Quand **est-ce que** vous retournez?	*When are you coming back?*
Comment **allez-vous?**	*How are you?*
Quel pays **est-ce que** tu préfères?	*Which country do you prefer?*

■ When prepositions are used with question words, they must precede them. (In English, they often appear at the end of a question.) **Que** becomes **quoi** after a preposition.

D'où Jeanne-Marie vient-elle?	*Where is Jeanne-Marie from?*
Sur quoi est-ce que nous écrivons?	*What are we writing about?*

C. Je n'ai pas entendu. Imagine you missed some of the information in each of the following statements. Complete the questions with the appropriate question word to get the information you missed. The information you didn't hear is in italics.

Modèle —Josette est *à Paris.*
➤ — <u>Où</u> est Josette?

1. —Il boit du thé *parce qu'il est enrhumé.*

   —_____ boit-il du thé?

2. —Hélène a *trois* sœurs.

   —_____ sœurs Hélène a-t-elle?

3. —Philippe et Louis sortent *avec des amies* ce soir.

   —_____ Philippe et Jean-Louis sortent-ils?

4. —Les voisins reçoivent *samedi soir.*

   —_____ les voisins reçoivent-ils?

5. —Elle travaille *bien.*

   —_____ travaille-t-elle?

6. —Je vais lire *ces* journaux *français.*

—_____ journaux vas-tu lire?

7. —Ils viennent *de Lyon.*

—_____ viennent-ils?

8. —*Charlotte* fait du sport.

—_____ fait du sport?

D. Les touristes posent des questions. A group of tourists is talking with their guide. His answers to their questions are negative, so they ask for clarification. Write what they say, asking for information about the words in italics.

Modèle —Nous allons descendre dans l'Hôtel *Marigny,* n'est-ce pas?
         —Non.
         ➤ —Dans quel hôtel est-ce que nous allons descendre, alors?

1. —Nous sortons par *cette porte,* n'est-ce pas?
   —Non.

   —_____

2. —Nous mangeons avec *les touristes anglais,* n'est-ce pas?
   —Non.

   —_____

3. —Le musée se trouve dans la rue *Napoléon,* n'est-ce pas?
   —Non.

   —_____

4. —Vous allez parler sur *l'histoire de cette ville,* n'est-ce pas?
   —Non.

   —_____

5. —On va mettre nos bagages dans *ce* taxi *noir,* n'est-ce pas?
   —Non.

   —_____

6. —Le train part de la Gare *de l'Ouest,* n'est-ce pas?
   —Non.

   —_____

➤➤➤➤➤

7. —Le message est pour *Olivier Durocher*, n'est-ce pas?

    —Non.

    — _____

8. —On va dîner chez *des familles françaises*, n'est-ce pas?

    —Non.

    — _____

III. More about Question Words

■ Notice the forms of **qui** and **que** with **est-ce que.**

1. To ask about people

qui est-ce qui? *or* **qui?**	*Who?* (subject of the sentence)
Qui est-ce qui chante? (**Qui** chante?)	*Who's singing?*
qui est-ce que?	*Whom?* (direct object of the verb)
Qui est-ce que tu connais ici?	*Whom do you know here?*

2. To ask about things or ideas

qu'est-ce qui?	*What?* (subject of the sentence)
Qu'est-ce qui intéresse les étudiants?	*What interests the students?*
qu'est-ce que? *or* **que?**	*What?* (direct object of the verb)
Qu'est-ce que tu veux manger?	*What do you want to eat?*
Que veux-tu manger?	*What do you want to eat?*

■ Inversion of the verb and subject pronoun is used to form information questions in formal French.

Quelle chanson **aimes-tu**?	*Which song do you like?*
Comment **allez-vous**?	*How are you?*
Combien de pages les étudiants **lisent-ils**?	*How many pages do the students read?*
Pourquoi ne **sortons-nous** pas?	*Why aren't we going out?*

■ When the subject of a short information question is a noun, inversion with a pronoun (**le chat mange-t-il?**) may be omitted. The noun is placed directly after the verb.

Que font **les enfants**?	*What are the children doing?*
Où travaille **ta mère**?	*Where does your mother work?*
Quand commence **le film**?	*When does the movie begin?*

This inversion of noun and verb is not possible after **pourquoi.** You may say either **Pourquoi est-ce que le professeur revient?** or **Pourquoi le professeur revient-il?**

■ In everyday French, question words may be placed at the end of a sentence to form an information question. **Que** and **qu'est-ce que** are replaced by **quoi** when they come at the end of a question.

Elle sort avec **qui**?	***Whom** is she going out with?*
Ils arrivent **quand**?	***When** are they getting here?*
Vous étudiez **quelle** matière?	***Which** subject are you studying?*
Ils cherchent **quoi**?	***What** are they looking for?*

E. **Enquête.** The police arrive at a Paris apartment after a robbery. They interview the residents. What information questions did the police ask to elicit the answers given? Write your questions in formal style using inversion.

Modèle   —Qu'a-t-on volé?
          —On a volé *des bijoux et de l'argent.*

Le vocabulaire du crime

le bijou *(pl.* **les bijoux**) *jewel*	**pousser un cri** *to cry out, utter a cry*
le cambrioleur *burglar*	**voler** *to steal*
le cri *shout*	**le voleur** *thief*

---

1. —_____
—Les cambrioleurs sont entrés dans l'appartement *à une heure.*

2. —_____
—Il y avait *deux* voleurs.

3. —_____
—Ils sont entrés *en ouvrant une fenêtre.*

4. —_____
—Les voleurs étaient *dans le salon.*

5. —_____
—Ils cherchaient *de l'argent.*

_____

➤➤➤➤➤

6. —_____

   —Nous avons téléphoné *à la police*.

7. —_____

   —*Ma femme* a poussé un cri.

8. —_____

   —Les cambrioleurs sont sortis par *la porte*.

F. On va aux magasins. Lucile et Corinne are talking about going shopping. Write Lucile's questions based on Corinne's answers. Use informal style for these information questions, placing the question word at the end.

Modèle   —Tu vas où?
   —Je vais *aux magasins*.

1. —_____

   —Je vais *cet après-midi*.

2. —_____

   —J'ai besoin *de vêtements*.

3. —_____

   —Je veux acheter *une jupe*.

4. —_____

   —Nous devons aller au magasin *«Élégance»*.

5. —_____

   —Je trouve ce magasin *splendide*.

6. —_____

   —Les jupes coûtent *300 francs*.

7. —_____

   —Le magasin ferme *à six heures*.

8. —_____

   —On peut aller au magasin *en autobus*.

IV. Other Types of Questions

■ The phrase **n'est-ce pas** can be added to statements to form a question to which the speaker expects the answer *yes*. Questions with **n'est-ce pas** are not real questions, but devices to ask for confirmation.

Il a une voiture, **n'est-ce pas?**   *He has a car, **doesn't he?***

Tes amis vont dîner en ville,   *Your friends are going to eat out,*
  n'est-ce pas?   ***aren't they?***

■ Negative sentences can also be turned into questions in French. The most common way to form a negative question in colloquial French is to say a negative sentence with rising intonation.

Les élèves ne sont pas **là?**   *Aren't the students **here?***

Vous n'allez pas voir **le film?**   *Aren't you going to see **the movie?***

■ Negative questions can also be formed with inversion. This construction is limited to formal language.

Les élèves **ne sont-ils pas** là?   ***Aren't** the students here?*

N'allez-vous pas voir le film?   ***Aren't** you going to see the movie?*

■ When answering *yes* to a negative question, **si** is used instead of **oui.**

—Tu **ne sors pas?**   *Aren't you going out?*
—**Si,** je sors maintenant.   ***Yes,** I'm going out now.*

G. Mais oui. Mais si. If you wanted to answer these questions with the word *yes*, would you use **oui** or **si?** Circle the correct response.

En voiture

faire une promenade en voiture *to go for a ride*

marcher *to work, to run (of cars, machines, etc.)*

le permis (de conduire) *driver's license*

la place *room, space*

---

1. Jean n'a pas de voiture?   Oui.   Si.

2. Il a son permis?   Oui.   Si.

3. Sa voiture ne marche pas?   Oui.   Si.

4. Il fait une promenade en voiture aujourd'hui?   Oui.   Si.

5. Tu vas avec lui?   Oui.   Si.

6. Il n'y a pas de place pour moi?   Oui.   Si.

H. Un nouvel étudiant. You're talking to a new student. What questions would you ask to get the following information? Since you are talking to a fellow student, use informal language: no inversion and question words at the end of the sentence.

1. You want to find out where the new student lives.

   _____

2. You want to know if he/she likes the *lycée*.

   _____

3. You want to know how many brothers and sisters he/she has.

   _____

4. You want to find out which sports he/she likes.

   _____

5. You want to know when he/she goes out.

   _____

6. You want to find out whom he/she goes out with.

   _____

7. You want to know what he/she's doing this weekend.

   _____

8. You want to find out how he/she gets home.

   _____

I. Composition. Create two dialogs, one between two students and one between two teachers. In both dialogs, the people are discussing their work and ask each other information questions and *yes/no* questions. The students should address each other as **tu** and use an informal style of question formation. The teachers should address each other as **vous** and use a formal style of question formation.

Negative Expressions and Indefinite Adjectives and Pronouns

I. Negative Sentences

The basic negative construction in French consists of **ne** before the verb and **pas** after it.

Nous **ne** travaillons **pas** aujourd'hui.   *We're **not** working today.*

■ Most negative constructions in French require **ne** before the verb and a negative word or expression after the verb. Review the following pairs of affirmative and negative words and expressions.

affirmative	negative
quelquefois *sometimes*	**jamais** *never*
souvent *often*	**jamais** *never*
quelqu'un *someone, somebody*	**personne** *no one, nobody*
quelque chose *something*	**rien** *nothing*
quelque part *somewhere*	**nulle part** *nowhere*
encore, davantage *more*	**plus** *no more*
soit... soit/soit... ou *either . . . or*	**ni... ni** *neither . . . nor*
déjà *already*	**pas encore** *not yet*

—Tu cherches **quelqu'un**?   *Are you looking for **somebody**?*
—Non, je **ne** cherche **personne**.   *No, I'm **not** looking for **anyone**.*

—Vous sortez **souvent** ensemble?   *Do you **often** go out together?*
—Non, je **ne** sors **jamais** avec eux.   *No, I **never** go out with them.*

■ Note that in contemporary French the word **déjà** often means *ever* as well as *already*, especially with the **passé composé.** Its negative counterpart is **jamais.**

—Tu as **déjà** visité la Tour Eiffel?   *Have you **ever** visited the Eiffel Tower?*

—Non, je **n'**y suis **jamais** allé.   *No, I've **never** gone there.*

■ The words **encore** and **toujours** often mean *still*. Their negative counterpart is **plus** *(no more, not any more)*.

—Elle travaille **encore** (**toujours**)   *Does she **still** work at the record store?*
au magasin de disques?
—Non, elle **n'**y travaille **plus**.   *No, she doesn't work there **any more**.*

■ There are some other words and expressions that serve as affirmative counterparts to negative expressions.

affirmative	negative
tout *everything*	**rien** *nothing*
tout le monde, tous *everyone*	**personne** *no one*
partout *everywhere*	**nulle part** *nowhere*
toujours *always*	**jamais** *never*

A. Une mauvaise attitude. Annette is in a bad mood today. She answers her friend's questions in the negative, using the appropriate negative word. Write out what she says.

Modèle   Tu es déjà prête?
➤ Non, je ne suis pas encore prête.

1. Tu invites quelqu'un?

   _____

2. Tu manges quelque chose?

   _____

3. Tu vas quelque part?

   _____

4. Tu vas quelquefois au cinéma?

   _____

5. Tu aimes encore les films d'aventure?

   _____

6. Tu veux aller soit au match soit au concert?

   _____

7. Tu as souvent envie de bavarder avec les copines?

   _____

B. Changement d'attitude! Annette is much cheerier and more sociable now. Describe the improvement in her attitude by answering these questions in the negative with the appropriate negative words.

Modèle   Est-ce qu'elle répond encore avec impatience?
        ➤ Non, elle ne répond plus avec impatience.

1. Est-ce qu'elle refuse encore de sortir?

   _____

2. Est-ce qu'elle est souvent fâchée?

   _____

3. Est-ce qu'elle est soit de mauvaise humeur soit triste?

   _____

4. Est-ce qu'elle reste toujours seule?

   _____

5. Est-ce qu'elle critique tout le monde?

   _____

6. Est-ce qu'elle mange toujours seule à la cantine?

   _____

C. Le mauvais étudiant. Luc and François are opposites. Luc is the perfect student; François is having difficulties at school. Describe François' problem by writing sentences that are the opposite of the ones about Luc. Use the appropriate affirmative or negative words.

Modèle   Luc arrive toujours à l'heure.
        ➤ François n'arrive jamais à l'heure.

1. Luc fait toujours ses devoirs.

   _____

2. Luc ne bavarde avec personne pendant la classe.

   _____

3. Luc va souvent à la bibliothèque.

   _____

➤➤➤➤➤

4. Luc n'interrompt jamais le professeur.

   _____

5. Luc écoute tout.

   _____

6. Luc ne dort jamais en classe.

   _____

7. Luc répond toujours aux questions du professeur.

   _____

8. Luc n'oublie rien à la maison.

   _____

D. Des changements profonds. Jean-Louis returns to his hometown after a 20-year absence. He runs into someone he knew who tells him about all the changes. Use **ne... plus** to describe them.

Modèle   ton ami Frédéric/habiter ici
   ➤ Ton ami Frédéric n'habite plus ici.

1. les Rousseau/avoir leur appartement rue de Dijon

   _____

2. Mme Delamarre/enseigner à l'école

   _____

3. la boulangerie de M. Courtillon/exister

   _____

4. le vieux M. Bouvard/vendre ses crêpes devant le théâtre

   _____

5. l'autobus/arrêter devant le cinéma

   _____

6. le train de Marseille/desservir *(serves)* notre ville

_____

7. le Café de la Place/rester ouvert toute la nuit

_____

8. on/jouer à la pétanque

_____

Traditions régionales

- A **crêpe** is a thin, pancake-like pastry, often filled with jam. It is a specialty of Brittany. Crêpes are often sold by street vendors.
- La **pétanque** is a game played by rolling metal balls toward a goal. It resembles the Italian game of bocci and is typical of southern France.
- Marseilles is France's third largest city, and the major Mediterranean port. Marseilles is an ancient city, founded as a trading post by Greeks in the sixth century B.C.

II. More about Negative Constructions

- After a negative, the indefinite articles **un, une, des** and the partitive articles **du, de la, de l', des** change to **de (d')**.

—Je vois que tu ne bois pas **de** bière.	*I see that you're not drinking any beer.*
—Je ne prends jamais **de** boissons alcoolisées.	*I never have alcoholic beverages.*

- The change of the indefinite and partitive articles to **de** does not take place when the verb is **être.**

—Ce n'est pas **un** violon, ça. C'est une petite guitare.	*That's not a violin. It's a little guitar.*
—Ces hommes ne sont pas **des** professeurs.	*Those men are not teachers.*

- The construction **ne... que** *(only)* is not a negative construction, and indefinite or partitive articles following **ne... que** do not change to **de**.

—Il n'écoute que **des** chansons.	*He listens only to songs.*
—Il n'aime que **de la** musique populaire.	*He likes only popular music.*

E. **La mode à l'école.** A new student is checking out what others wear at her new school. Answer her questions in the negative. Follow the model.

Modèle —Est-ce qu'on porte des jeans?
➤ —Non, on ne porte pas de jeans.

1. —Est-ce que tu portes des lunettes de soleil en classe, toi?

   _____

2. —Est-ce que les étudiants mettent des chapeaux?

   _____

3. —Est-ce qu'on porte des bottes?

   _____

4. —Est-ce que tu mets un bonnet de laine en hiver?

   _____

5. —Est-ce qu'on voit des imperméables au printemps?

   _____

6. —Est-ce qu'on porte des écharpes?

   _____

F. **Quel café!** A group of students on a hike has stopped at a café. Unfortunately, the café doesn't have any of the things they want to eat or drink. Write the waiter's answers to each of the student's requests following the model.

Modèle —Pour moi, une limonade, s'il vous plaît.
➤ —Nous n'avons pas de limonade.

1. —Je voudrais un sandwich au fromage.

   _____

2. —Des croissants, s'il vous plaît.

   _____

3. —Donnez-moi un thé, s'il vous plaît.

   _____

4. —Vous avez des glaces?

   _____

5. —Vous avez des jus de fruit?

_____

6. —Pour moi, une soupe à l'oignon, s'il vous plaît.

_____

7. —Nous voudrions manger des pâtisseries.

_____

G. Seulement cela. You are in a restaurant questioning the waiter about the menu. In each case he answers that the restaurant has only one of the two things you mention, the item in italics. Write the waiter's responses using **ne... que** following the model.

Modèle   —Vous avez des anchois et *des crevettes?*
      ➤ —Nous n'avons que des crevettes.

Au restaurant

les anchois *(masc. pl.) anchovies*

les crevettes *(fem. pl.) shrimp*

les crustacés *(masc. pl.) shellfish*

la purée de pommes de terre *mashed potatoes*

---

1. —Vous avez du poulet et *de la viande?*

— _____

2. —Vous faites *des frites* et de la purée de pommes de terre?

— _____

3. —Vous servez du veau et *de l'agneau?*

— _____

4. —Vous avez *du poisson* et des crustacés?

— _____

5. —Vous préparez des soupes et *des salades?*

— _____

6. —Vous servez *des vins français* et des vins étrangers?

— _____

III. More Negative Constructions

■ When **rien** or **personne** is the subject of a sentence, it precedes the verb. **Ne** is placed before the verb (after **rien** and **personne**) as in all other negative constructions.

—**Rien n'**est prêt.	*Nothing is ready.*
—C'est que **personne ne** travaille.	*That's because **no one** works.*

■ The negative expression corresponding to **aussi** is **non plus** *(neither)*. **Non plus** usually refers to the subject of the sentence and is often used with the stressed pronouns.

—Caroline n'aime pas cette chanson.	*Caroline doesn't like this song.*
—Maurice **non plus**.	*Neither does Maurice./Maurice doesn't **either**.*
—Je ne comprends pas.	*I don't understand.*
—Moi **non plus**.	*Neither do I.*
—Nous ne pouvons pas sortir aujourd'hui.	*We can't go out today.*
—Ni eux **non plus**.	*Neither can they.*

■ To negate a noun, French uses **ne... aucun(e)**. Although the noun after **aucun(e)** is always singular in French, the English equivalent often has a plural noun.

—Ce prof **n'**explique **aucun** problème.	*This teacher does**n't** explain **any** problems.*
—Pourquoi?	*Why?*
—Je **n'**ai **aucune** idée.	*I have **no** idea.*

■ A noun preceded by **aucun** can also be the subject of a sentence. **Ne** precedes the verb.

Aucun étudiant **n'**aime cette classe.	*No student likes this class.*

■ **Aucun** and **aucune** can also precede a prepositional phrase beginning with **de.** In this construction they are pronouns.

—Tu **ne** lis **aucun de** ces livres.	*You're **not** reading **any** of those books.*
—**Aucune des** histoires **n'**est intéressante.	*None of the stories is interesting.*

■ To make a more emphatic negative you can use **pas du tout** instead of **pas.**

Ma mère **n'**est **pas du tout** contente.	*My mother is**n't at all** happy.*

■ **Pas** can be used to negate other parts of speech such as nouns and stressed pronouns.

—Tu viens jeudi?	*Are you coming on Thursday?*
—**Pas** jeudi, vendredi.	*Not on Thursday, on Friday.*
—On va à la bibliothèque?	*Shall we go to the library?*
—**Pas** moi.	*Not I.*

■ Here are some negative expressions that can be used along with or instead of **non** as responses.

Pas du tout.	*Not at all.*
Absolument pas.	*Absolutely not. Definitely not.*
En aucun cas.	*Under no circumstances.*
Ce n'est pas vrai.	*Wrong. Not true.*
Jamais de la vie!	*Never!*

H. De mauvais étudiants. Mlle Richard, the French teacher, is complaining about one of her French classes. Write out what she says using **personne** as the subject of each sentence.

Modèle   écouter ➤ Personne n'écoute.

1. arriver à l'heure _____

2. faire attention _____

3. comprendre _____

4. répondre _____

5. prendre des notes _____

6. étudier _____

I. La paresse. Mlle Richard's colleague, Mlle Laval, has a lazy class. Write out her complaints about her students using **aucun(e).** Remember that **aucun(e)** is followed by a singular noun.

Modèle   faire les devoirs ➤ Ils ne font aucun devoir.

1. écrire des rédactions

   _____

2. conjuguer des verbes

   _____

3. répéter des phrases

   _____

4. comprendre des explications

   _____

5. répondre à des questions

   _____

J. **Les projets au négatif.** Summarize what people are *not* doing during their vacations using **non plus** as in the model.

Modèle   Moi, je ne reste pas ici. Toi, tu ne restes pas ici.
➤ Moi, je ne reste pas ici. Toi non plus.

1. Luc ne va pas au bord de la mer. Alain ne va pas au bord de la mer.

_____

2. Toi, tu ne voyages pas. Nous, nous ne voyageons pas.

_____

3. Serge ne veut pas aller à la montagne. Vous, vous ne voulez pas aller à la montagne.

_____

4. Nous n'allons pas en Bretagne. Eux, ils ne vont pas en Bretagne.

_____

5. Charles ne suit pas de cours. Moi, je ne suis pas de cours.

_____

6. Lucie ne va pas à l'étranger. Vincent et Lise ne vont pas à l'étranger.

_____

IV. Indefinite Adjective and Pronouns; *tout*

■ *Some* before a noun is expressed by the partitive article in French, or by **quelques** *(some, a few)* before a plural noun.

—J'ai acheté **quelques** journaux.   *I bought **a few (some)** newspapers.*

■ *Some* as a pronoun is expressed by **quelques-uns, quelques-unes** and usually appears with the object pronoun **en.**

—Tu as reçu des cadeaux?   *Did you get any gifts?*
—Oui, j'**en** ai reçu **quelques-uns.**   *Yes, I got **some** (= a few).*

—Tu écris des lettres?   *Are you writing any letters?*
—J'**en** écris **quelques-unes.**   *I'm writing **some**.*

■ Indefinite words (and their negative counterparts) are followed by the word **de** before an adjective. The adjective is always masculine singular.

—Y a-t-il quelque chose **d'**intéressant   *Is there anything interesting on T.V.?*
à la télé?
—Non, rien **de** bon.   *No, nothing good.*

■ The word **tout** can be both an adjective and a pronoun in French. As an adjective **tout** has four forms.

	singular	plural
masculine	tout	tous
feminine	toute	toutes

■ **Tout** is different from other adjectives in that it precedes the definite article. As a singular adjective it means *all, the whole*.

tout le travail	*all the work*
toute la ville	*the whole city*

■ As a plural adjective **tous, toutes** mean *every, all*. **Tou(te)s les deux** means *both*.

tous les livres	*all (the) books, every book*
toutes les revues	*all (the) magazines, every magazine*

■ **Tout** as a pronoun means *everything*. It takes a third-person singular verb form when it is the subject of the sentence.

Tout va bien?	*Is everything all right?*

■ **Tous** (final **s** pronounced) means *everyone, everybody*. It takes a third-person plural (**ils/elles**) verb form when it is the subject of the sentence.

Tous vont arriver à midi.	*Everyone (or: All of them) will arrive at noon.*

■ *Everyone* is more commonly expressed by the phrase **tout le monde,** which takes a third-person *singular* (**il/elle**) verb form when it is the subject of the sentence.

Tout le monde aime ce professeur.	*Everyone likes this teacher.*

K. À refaire. Combine each pair of sentences into a single one using the word **de.**

Modèle Je connais quelqu'un. Elle est gentille.
➤ Je connais quelqu'un de gentil.

1. Tu veux manger quelque chose? Voici des tartes exquises.

_____

2. Dans ce magasin il n'y a rien. Rien n'est joli.

_____

3. Il faut chercher quelqu'un. Il doit être intelligent.

_____

➤➤➤➤➤

4. Il n'y a personne ici. Personne n'est patient.

   _____

5. Je ne trouve rien dans cet article. Rien n'est intéressant.

   _____

6. Il faut chercher quelque chose. Il faut chercher une chose nouvelle.

   _____

L. Seulement quelques-un. In each of these cases, there are only a few of the things asked about. Say so using **quelques-un(e)s** and putting **en** before the verb. Follow the model.

Modèle —Tu as des crayons?
   ➤ —J'en ai quelques-uns.

1. —Tu lis des revues?

   — _____

2. —Tu veux des frites?

   — _____

3. —Tu écoutes des compact-disques?

   — _____

4. —Tu reçois des paquets?

   — _____

5. —Tu achètes des sandwichs?

   — _____

M. À compléter. Complete the following sentences about a typical school day of Christine's with **tout, toute, tous, toutes,** as required.

1. _____ les étudiants arrivent à huit heures.

2. Ils attendent _____ dans la cour.

3. _____ les classes commencent à huit heures dix.

4. Nous déjeunons _____ à midi.

5. _____ la cantine est pleine.

6. Nous mangeons _____ ensemble.

7. _____ mes copines rentrent avec moi à trois heures.

8. _____ le monde fait ses devoirs avant de dîner.

N. Questions personnelles. Answer the following questions in complete French sentences.

1. Est-ce que vous avez un vélo tout terrain?

_____

2. Qu'est-ce qu'il y a de bon à la cantine?

_____

3. Est-ce que vous avez avec vous un parapluie et un imperméable?

_____

4. Est-ce qu'on porte des maillots de bain en classe?

_____

5. Est-ce que tout le monde est sympathique à votre école?

_____

O. Composition. Make lists of complete sentences that describe three things you (or you and your friends) never do on weekends, three things you don't do any more at school, and three things that you don't have any of. Use the appropriate negative constructions.

CHAPTER 11

Object Pronouns

I. Direct Object Pronouns

■ In French, if the object is connected to its verb without a preposition, it is called a *direct object*. If the object is connected to its verb with a preposition, it is called an *indirect object*. Thus, in the sentence **Je vois Paul, Paul** is the direct object of **vois.** In the sentence **Je téléphone à Paul, Paul** is the indirect object of the verb **téléphone.**

Direct object nouns can be replaced by direct object pronouns.

DIRECT OBJECT PRONOUNS

singular	plural
me, m' *me*	**nous** *us*
te, t' *you*	**vous** *you*
le, l' *him, it*	**les** *them*
la, l' *her, it*	

■ In English, direct object pronouns follow the verb, while in French they come before it. If the verb begins with a vowel, **m'** replaces **me, t'** replaces **te,** and **l'** replaces **le** and **la.**

—Tu aimes ces chaussures?   *Do you like these shoes?*
—Non, je ne **les** aime pas du tout.   *No, I don't like **them** at all.*

—Quand est-ce que tu écris la lettre?   *When are you writing the letter?*
—Je **l'**écris demain.   *I'm writing **it** tomorrow.*

—Tu **m'**invites?   *Are you treating me?*
—Oui, je **t'**invite.   *Yes, I'll treat **you.***

■ In verb + infinitive constructions, the object pronoun is placed before the *infinitive.*

—Je peux mettre ce compact disque?   *May I put on this compact disc?*
Je ne veux pas **te** déranger.   *I don't want to bother **you.***
—Oui, tu peux **le** mettre. Tu ne   *Yes, you can put **it** on. You're not*
vas pas **me** déranger.   *going to bother **me.***

In the negative, the **ne** precedes the object pronoun with a single verb.

Le cinéma? Je ne **le** vois pas.   *The movie theatre? I don't see **it.***

■ In verb + infinitive constructions, the first verb is usually made negative and the object pronoun precedes the infinitive, coming after the negative word.

Ces gants? Je ne vais pas **les** acheter.   *Those gloves? I'm not going to buy* ***them.***

■ Several verbs that take indirect objects in English take direct objects in French. (In the examples in this chapter, the abbreviation **qqch** means **quelque chose** and stands for any noun referring to a thing and the abbreviation **qqn** means **quelqu'un** and stands for any noun referring to a person.)

attendre qqn/qqch *to wait for someone/something*

chercher qqn/qqch *to look for someone/something*

demander qqch *to ask for something*

écouter qqn/qqch *to listen to someone/something*

regarder qqn/qqch *to look at someone/something*

The verb **payer** also takes a direct object in French, so **payer qqch** means *to pay for something.*

—Qui va payer **les billets**?	*Who's going to pay for **the tickets**?*
—Moi, je vais **les** payer.	*I'm going to pay for **them**.*

A. La voiture de Philippe. Philippe is a careful driver and takes good care of his new car. Tell what he does by answering the questions with the verb in parentheses and the appropriate direct object pronoun.

Modèle   —Et les vitres? *(nettoyer)*
          ➢ —Il les nettoie.

La voiture

le capot *hood (car)*	**le pneu** *tire;* **le pneu crevé** *flat tire*
la ceinture de sécurité *seat belt*	**la portière** *car door*
le frein *brake*	**le réservoir** *gas tank*
l'huile *(fem.) oil*	**vérifier le niveau de l'huile**
le niveau *level*	*to check the oil*
les phares *(masc. pl.) headlights*	**le vitre** *car window*

---

1. —Et le niveau de l'huile? *(vérifier)*

   — _____

2. —Et les phares? *(mettre la nuit)*

   — _____

3. —Et le pneu crevé? *(changer)*

   — _____

4. —Et la ceinture de sécurité? *(mettre toujours)*

   — _____

➢➢➢➢➢

5. —Et le capot? *(ouvrir)*

   —_____

6. —Et la portière? *(fermer)*

   —_____

7. —Et les freins? *(réparer)*

   —_____

B. Le match de football. Pierre and his friends are soccer fans. Tell how they get to see a game by adding to each sentence another one consisting of the subject and verb indicated plus the appropriate object pronoun.

Modèle   Pierre achète le journal pour voir s'il y a un match. *(il/lire)*
   ➤ Il le lit.

1. Il y a une annonce dans le journal. *(il/chercher)*

   _____

2. Le match se joue dans un stade de la banlieue. *(il/connaître)*

   _____

3. Jean-Paul et Louis veulent voir le match aussi. *(Pierre/inviter)*

   _____

4. Il faut acheter les billets. *(Pierre/prendre)*

   _____

5. Il faut prendre l'autobus pour aller au stade. *(les garçons/attendre)*

   _____

6. Quand ils arrivent au stade, ils cherchent leurs places. *(ils/trouver)*

   _____

C. Une étudiante en difficulté. Madeleine is having problems at school. Use the verbs in parentheses and the appropriate object pronouns to tell why she is falling behind.

Modèle   Elle a des devoirs. *(ne pas/faire)* ➤ Elle ne les fait pas.

1. Elle a un bon professeur. *(ne pas/écouter)*

   _____

2. Le professeur donne des explications. *(ne pas/comprendre)*

_____

3. Les autres étudiants font attention. *(déranger)*

_____

4. Elle a de bons livres. *(ne pas/ouvrir)*

_____

5. Chaque étudiant doit avoir un stylo. *(oublier à la maison)*

_____

6. Les étudiants ont des articles à lire. *(ne pas/lire)*

_____

D. **Le va-et-vient.** Answer each of these questions either affirmatively or negatively, as indicated with the appropriate object pronoun. Consider **vous** a plural rather than a formal singular.

Modèle   —Tu peux m'accompagner? *(non)*
           ➤ —Non, je ne peux pas t'accompagner.

Le va-et-vient (Comings and goings)

contacter qqn *to get in touch with someone*

déposer qqn *to drop someone off*

emmener qqn *to take someone (somewhere)*

prendre qqn *to pick someone up (to take him/her somewhere)*

quitter qqn *to leave someone*

raccompagner qqn *to take someone home*

1. Vous pouvez nous déposer en ville? *(oui)*

_____

2. Je dois te quitter? *(oui)*

_____

3. Tu veux m'emmener? *(non)*

_____

➤➤➤➤➤

4. Vous venez nous prendre? *(non)*

_____

5. Tu peux me raccompagner? *(oui)*

_____

6. Vous comptez nous contacter? *(oui)*

_____

II. Indirect Object Pronouns

■ Indirect objects indicate the person *to whom* or *for whom* an action is done. They are connected to the verb by the preposition **à.**

Nous parlons **à** nos amis.	*We speak **to** our friends.*
J'écris **à** mes cousins en Californie.	*I write **to** my cousins in California.*
Je prête ma bicyclette **à** mon frère.	*I lend my bicycle **to** my brother.*

■ French indirect object pronouns refer only to people. Note that the indirect object pronouns are the same as the direct object pronouns for **je, tu, nous,** and **vous** forms. In the **il/elle** form, **lui** means both *to him* and *to her,* depending on the noun it refers to.

INDIRECT OBJECT PRONOUNS

singular	plural
me, m' *to/for me*	**nous** *to/for us*
te, t' *to/for you*	**vous** *to/for you*
lui *to/for him/her*	**leur** *to/for them*

■ Like direct object pronouns, indirect object pronouns precede a single conjugated verb.

—Tu écris à tes cousins ou tu **leur** téléphones?	*Do you write to your cousins or do you phone **them**?*
—Je **leur** écris.	*I write (to) **them**.*

■ And like direct object pronouns, they precede the infinitive in verb + infinitive constructions.

—Qu'est-ce que tu vas **lui** offrir pour son anniversaire?	*What are you going to give **her** for her birthday?*
—Je veux **lui** offrir un foulard en soie.	*I want to give **her** a silk scarf.*

- Some verbs that take indirect objects in French have other constructions in English.

    obéir à qqn *to obey someone* (and **désobéir à** qqn *to disobey someone*)

    répondre à qqn *to answer someone*

    téléphoner à qqn *to call, phone someone*

- Note also the following common verbal expressions that take an indirect object.

    aller bien à qqn *to look nice on someone*

    Ce chemisier **te** va très bien.   *That blouse looks nice on **you.***

    plaire à qqn *to please someone, to like*

    Ce restaurant **leur** plaît.   ***They** like this restaurant. (It pleases **them.**)*

E. Des solutions. Each of these people wants or needs something done. Tell who is going to help and how using the subject and verb in parentheses plus the appropriate indirect object pronoun.

Modèle   Janine veut voir les photos. *(sa mère/montrer les photos)*
➤ Sa mère lui montre les photos.

1. Odile a besoin d'un foulard en soie. *(son petit ami/offrir un foulard en soie)*

   _____

2. Maurice veut étudier pour l'examen de biologie. *(je/rendre son livre)*

   _____

3. Nicole et Albert n'ont pas de calculatrice. *(nous/prêter nos calculatrices)*

   _____

4. Moi, je ne sais pas la réponse. *(toi/dire la réponse)*

   _____

5. Mon père cherche une voiture d'occasion. *(le voisin/vendre sa vieille voiture)*

   _____

6. Charles et son frère n'ont rien à lire. *(nous/apporter des revues)*

   _____

7. Mes grands-parents veulent savoir si tout va bien. *(je/écrire une lettre)*

   _____

F. Je ne sais pas. Answer each question saying that you don't know if you are going to do the things asked about or if the things are going to happen. Replace the indirect objects in italics with the appropriate pronouns.

Modèle —Tu vas montrer ces photos *à tes copains*?
➤ —Je ne sais pas si je vais leur montrer ces photos.

1. —Tu vas répondre *à Sandrine*?

   — _____

2. —Tu vas téléphoner *à tes cousins*?

   — _____

3. —Tu vas *me* prêter ta bicyclette?

   — _____

4. —Tu vas envoyer un cadeau *à ta tante en Europe*?

   — _____

5. —Est-ce qu'on va *t'*offrir un vélo tout terrain pour ton anniversaire?

   — _____

6. —Tu vas *me* rendre mes notes aujourd'hui?

   — _____

III. The Pronoun *y*

■ The indirect objects **lui** and **leur** replace a phrase consisting of the preposition **à** + an animate noun (a noun referring to a person). The pronoun **y** replaces a phrase consisting of the preposition **à** + an inanimate noun (a noun referring to a *thing*). There are various possible equivalents of **y** in English. **Y** can mean *it* or *them*.

—Les étudiants répondent **aux questions**?	*Do the students answer **the questions**?*
—Oui, ils **y** répondent. (**y** = aux questions)	*Yes, they answer **them**.*

■ **Y** can be the equivalent of various prepositions followed by *it* or *them*.

—Tu penses **à l'examen**?	*Are you thinking about **the test**?*
—Non, je n'**y** pense pas. (**y** = à l'examen)	*No, I'm not thinking about **it**.*

■ **Y** can also replace phrases consisting of a preposition of location such as **à, en, dans, sur, sous, devant, derrière** + a noun of place. In this usage, **y** often means *there.*

> Je vais **à Paris.** J'**y** travaille.   *I'm going **to Paris.** I work **there.***
> (**y** = à Paris)
>
> Le chat est **sous la chaise.** Il **y** dort.   *The cat is **under the chair.** He sleeps*
> (**y** = sous la chaise)   ***there.***

G. C'est pour ça! Explain the consequences of each of these situations using the cues given and the pronoun **y.**

Modèle   Cette question est très difficile. *(les étudiants/ne pas pouvoir/répondre)*
➤ C'est pour ça que les étudiants ne peuvent pas y répondre.

1. Ce parc est joli et tranquille. *(je/aller/rester un peu plus)*

   _____

2. Marc dit que cette table est sale. *(il/ne pas vouloir/laisser ses affaires)*

   _____

3. Cette boucherie est excellente. *(je/compter/acheter toute ma viande)*

   _____

4. Cet immeuble est très joli. *(vous/devoir/chercher un appartement)*

   _____

5. Le cinéma est à huit kilomètres d'ici. *(nous/ne pas pouvoir/aller à pied)*

   _____

6. Les examens vont être trop difficiles. *(il ne faut pas/penser)*

   _____

7. On dit que le concert ne va pas être bon. *(je/ne pas vouloir/aller)*

   _____

IV. The Pronoun *en*

■ The pronoun **en** replaces phrases consisting of **de** + noun. In most cases it can replace both animate and inanimate nouns. **En** very often replaces the partitive **de** or the plural indefinite article **des**.

—Tu as **de l'argent**?　　　　　　　*Do you have **any money**?*
—Non, je n'**en** ai pas. (pas **d'argent**)　　*No, I don't have **any**.*

—Tu lis **des romans policiers**?　　*Do you read **detective novels**?*
—Oui, j'**en** lis.　　　　　　　　　*Yes, I do. (= Yes, I read **some**.)*

■ **En** is also commonly used to replace nouns that appear after quantity words such as **beaucoup, trop, assez** or after numbers.

—Tu as combien **d'examens** cette　　*How many **tests** do you have this year?*
　année?
—J'**en** ai trop. (**en** = d'examens)　　*I have too many.*
—Moi, j'**en** ai quatre.　　　　　　*I have four (**of them**).*
—Tu **en** as beaucoup, mais moi,　　*You have a lot, but I have six!*
　j'**en** ai six!

■ **En** also replaces phrases consisting of **de** + a noun of place. Its English equivalent is *from there*.

—Marc est toujours à Paris?　　　　*Is Marc still in Paris?*
—Oui. Il **en** revient vendredi.　　　*Yes, he's coming back (**from there**)*
　(**en** = de Paris)　　　　　　　　*on Friday.*

When the pronoun **en** is added to the phrase **il y a** it becomes **il y en a**.

—Est-ce qu'il y a des étudiants　　　*Are there any foreign students in*
　étrangers dans votre lycée?　　　　*your high school?*
—Oui, **il y en a** beaucoup.　　　　*Yes, **there are many** (**of them**).*

H. Pour être un peu plus précis. Marcelle is discussing her wardrobe with her friend Chantal. Write out Marcelle's answers to Chantal's questions using the quantity word in parentheses and the pronoun **en**.

Modèle —Tu as des foulards? *(beaucoup)*
　　　　➤ —J'en ai beaucoup.

Les vêtements

les collants *(masc. pl.) panty hose*　　la manche *sleeve;* à manches
démodé *out of fashion*　　　　　　　　courtes *short-sleeved*
essayer (j'essaie) *to try on*　　　　　　le pull *sweater*

---

1. —Tu achètes des collants? *(beaucoup)*

　— _____

2. —Tu as des robes démodées? *(très peu)*

   — _____

3. —Tu cherches des bikinis pour l'été? *(quelques-uns)*

   — _____

4. —Tu essaies des pulls aux magasins? *(trop)*

   — _____

5. —Tu as des chemisiers pour l'hiver? *(assez)*

   — _____

6. —Tu as un anorak? *(deux)*

   — _____

7. —Tu as des chemisiers à manches courtes? *(plusieurs)*

   — _____

I. **Un de plus.** Laurent wants to know about Rachel's school. She answers that in each case there is one more than Laurent thinks. Write out her answers using the pronoun **en.**

Modèle —Tu as huit matières?
➤ —J'en ai neuf.

1. —Il y a 20 étudiants dans ta classe de géographie?

   — _____

2. —Est-ce que tu lis dix romans par an?

   — _____

3. —Est-ce que tu rédiges une rédaction par semaine?

   — _____

4. —Est-ce que tu fais une langue étrangère?

   — _____

5. —Est-ce que les étudiants écoutent une cassette par jour?

   — _____

6. —Est-ce que vous écrivez deux dissertations par semestre?

   — _____

J. Joseph va en France. Summarize Joseph's trip to France by replacing the nouns in italics by the appropriate object pronouns.

Modèle   Joseph aime la France. Il veut passer ses vacances *en France.*
➤ Joseph aime la France. Il veut y passer ses vacances.

1. Il veut aller avec son ami Roger. Il téléphone *à Roger.*

   Il veut aller avec son ami Roger. _____

2. Roger aime l'idée d'un voyage en France. Il veut faire *ce voyage* cet été.

   Roger aime l'idée d'un voyage en France. _____

3. Ils veulent parler avec le Bureau de Tourisme à New York. Ils téléphonent *au Bureau.*

   Ils veulent parler avec le Bureau de Tourisme à New York.

   _____

4. Ils demandent des brochures touristiques. Ils reçoivent beaucoup *de brochures.*

   Ils demandent des brochures touristiques. _____

5. Il faut prendre des billets d'avion. Ils prennent *leurs billets* à l'agence de voyage.

   Il faut prendre des billets d'avion. _____

6. Ils vont à New York. Ils prennent l'avion *à New York.*

   Ils vont à New York. _____

7. Ils passent l'été en France. Ils reviennent *de France* en septembre.

   Ils passent l'été en France. _____

L'aviation et le tourisme

- The main French airlines are **Air France** for international flights and **Air Inter** for flights within France. Air France is one of the world's major airlines, serving nearly 200 cities in 75 countries. The Paris airports of **Orly** and **Roissy-Charles de Gaulle** are major transfer points in Europe for air travelers, with over 50 million travelers a year.
- The French government maintains tourist offices in major cities around the world where people can get information about traveling to France. These offices offer a variety of printed information and the opportunity to speak with travel specialists.

V. Double Object Pronouns

- When two object pronouns appear in the same sentence, they are placed in the following order.

DOUBLE OBJECT PRONOUNS

me				
te	le, l'			
se before	la, l' before	lui, leur before	y before	en
nous	les			
vous				

- Double object pronouns follow the same rules of placement as single object pronouns. The object pronouns **me, te, se, le, la** become **m', t', s', l'** before **y** and **en.**

—Quand envoies-tu les **cadeaux**
  à **Michel?**
—Je **les lui** envoie aujourd'hui.

*When are you sending **Michel the**
  gifts?*
*I'm sending **them to him** today.*

—Nous n'avons pas **de cassettes.**
—Je peux **vous en** prêter.

*We don't have any **cassettes.***
*I can lend **you some.***

K. Combien? Answer each of the following questions using an indirect object pronoun + **en** and the cue in parentheses that indicates the amount. The words in italics should be replaced in your answers.

Modèle   —Combien *de lettres* est-ce que tu écris *à ton frère?*
          (deux par semaine)
     ➤ —Je lui en écris deux par semaine.

1. —Combien *de conseils* est-ce que le professeur *vous* donne? *(trop)*

   — _____

2. —Combien *de pages de lecture* est-ce que le professeur demande *aux étudiants?* (80)

   — _____

3. —Combien *de livres* est-ce que tu prêtes *à Sophie?* *(huit)*

   — _____

4. —Combien *de photos* est-ce que Sylvie va *nous* montrer? *(beaucoup)*

   — _____

5. —Combien *d'affiches* est-ce que tu comptes donner *à Julien?* *(cinq)*

   — _____

➤➤➤➤➤

6. —Combien *de plats* est-ce que vous allez *nous* servir? *(trois)*

    —_____

7. —Combien *de problèmes* est-ce que le professeur va *nous* expliquer? *(dix)*

    —_____

L. Qu'est-ce qu'il faut faire? Using a direct and an indirect object with the expression **il faut** and the cue in parentheses, tell what has to be done in each of these situations.

Modèle   Jacques a besoin de son livre d'allemand. *(rendre)*
➤ Il faut le lui rendre.

1. Nos cousins au Canada veulent voir les photos de nos vacances. *(envoyer)*

    _____

2. Olivier ne sait pas l'adresse de Christine. *(dire)*

    _____

3. Les voisins veulent acheter notre vieille voiture. *(vendre)*

    _____

4. Vincent a nos billets pour le match. *(demander)*

    _____

5. Le prof veut voir ma dissertation. *(donner)*

    _____

6. Monique et Chantal veulent voir nos nouveaux vêtements. *(montrer)*

    _____

7. Stéphane n'a pas les 300 francs pour acheter ses livres. *(prêter)*

    _____

M. Questions personnelles. Answer each question in a complete French sentence, replacing the italicized words by object pronouns in your answers.

1. Est-ce que vous retrouvez *vos amis devant l'école?*

   _____

2. Est-ce que vos professeurs *vous* expliquent *les choses difficiles?*

   _____

3. Combien *de pages de lecture* avez-vous par semaine?

   _____

4. Est-ce que vous envoyez souvent *des messages électroniques à vos amis?*

   _____

5. Est-ce que vous montrez *vos examens à vos parents?*

   _____

N. Composition. Write about gifts you have given and received. Tell about where you bought the gifts and what the people's reactions were. Talk about your reactions to presents given to you.

The *passé composé*

I. The *passé composé* with *avoir*

■ French uses the tense called **passé composé** to express actions completed in the past.

Monsieur Dupont **a fait** ses valises, **a appelé** un taxi, et **a fermé** la porte à clé.	*Monsieur Dupont **packed** his bags, **called** a taxi, and **locked** the door.*

■ The **passé composé** is a two-part verb consisting of the auxiliary verb **avoir** followed by the past participle. (Some verbs use **être** as the auxiliary verb. These will be presented in section III.)

■ Here is the conjugation of **parler**.

PASSÉ COMPOSÉ OF PARLER

j'**ai parlé** *I spoke*	nous **avons parlé** *we spoke*
tu **as parlé** *you spoke*	vous **avez parlé** *you spoke*
il/elle **a parlé** *he/she/it spoke*	ils/elles **ont parlé** *they spoke*
on **a parlé** *people/they/we spoke*	

■ The past participle of regular verbs is formed by replacing the infinitive endings as follows:

-**er** verbs change -**er** to -**é**	**parler** ➤ **parlé**
-**ir** verbs change -**ir** to -**i**	**finir** ➤ **fini**
-**re** verbs change -**re** to -**u**	**vendre** ➤ **vendu**

■ Many common verbs have irregular past participles.

apprendre *to learn* ➤ **appris**	**écrire** *to write* ➤ **écrit**
avoir *to have* ➤ **eu**	**être** *to be* ➤ **été**
boire *to drink* ➤ **bu**	**faire** *to make, do* ➤ **fait**
comprendre *to understand* ➤ **compris**	**lire** *to read* ➤ **lu**
connaître *to know* ➤ **connu**	**mettre** *to put, place* ➤ **mis**
construire *to construct* ➤ **construit**	**ouvrir** *to open* ➤ **ouvert**
courir *to run* ➤ **couru**	**pouvoir** *to be able to, can* ➤ **pu**
couvrir *to cover* ➤ **couvert**	**prendre** *to take* ➤ **pris**
croire *to believe* ➤ **cru**	**produire** *to produce* ➤ **produit**
découvrir *to discover* ➤ **découvert**	**recevoir** *to receive* ➤ **reçu**
devoir *to be obliged to* ➤ **dû**	**savoir** *to know* ➤ **su**
dire *to say, tell* ➤ **dit**	**souffrir** *to suffer* ➤ **souffert**

suivre *to follow* ➤ suivi   voir *to see* ➤ vu

tenir *to hold, keep* ➤ tenu   vouloir *to want* ➤ voulu

venir *to come* ➤ venu

Nous **avons ouvert** la chambre et y   *We **opened** the room and **put** the*
 avons mis le chat.   *cat there.*

A. Qu'est-ce qu'ils ont fait? Tell what these friends' day in the country
 (**à la campagne**) was like by rewriting each of the sentences in the **passé
 composé.**

Modèle   Les copains décident de passer une journée à la campagne.
 ➤ Les copains ont décidé de passer une journée à la campagne.

1. Sandrine et Marie font des sandwichs.

   _____

2. Luc et Maurice achètent de l'eau minérale.

   _____

3. Charles et Paulette cherchent un ballon.

   _____

4. Moi, je prends la voiture de mon père.

   _____

5. Nous découvrons un joli endroit à côté du fleuve.

   _____

6. Nous mangeons avec beaucoup d'appétit.

   _____

7. On joue au football.

   _____

8. Toi, tu apportes ta guitare.

   _____

9. Tout le monde chante ensemble.

   _____

10. Nous passons une journée merveilleuse.

   _____

II. The Negative and Interrogative of the *passé composé*

■ To form the negative of the **passé composé,** place **ne** before the form of **avoir** and **pas** after it.

—Tu **n'as pas encore** préparé le déjeuner?   *You haven't prepared lunch **yet**?*

—Non, j'ai regardé la télé.   *No, I watched TV.*

■ Most other negative words are placed after the form of **avoir** and before the past participle, like **pas.**

—Et ta dissertation? Tu **n'as rien** écrit!   *What about your paper? You haven't written **anything**.*

—Je **n'ai jamais** eu tant de difficulté.   *I've **never** had so much trouble.*

■ The negative words **personne** and **nulle part** *follow* the past participle.

—Tu as cherché ton copain?   *Did you look for your friend?*

—Oui, mais je **n'ai** vu **personne.**   *Yes, but I didn't see **anyone**.*

■ When inversion is used to ask a question in the **passé composé,** the auxiliary and the subject pronoun are inverted. The pronoun **je** is not usually inverted in questions.

—**As-tu** mangé?   ***Have you** eaten?*

—**A-t-on** déjà servi le déjeuner?   ***Have they** already served lunch?*

B. Ce qu'ils n'ont pas fait. A group of friends is discussing what they haven't done. Write what they say by creating sentences from each string of elements using the **passé composé.** Be sure to place negative words in their correct position.

Modèle   Robert/acheter une voiture/pas encore
      ➤ Robert n'a pas encore acheté de voiture.

1. Sophie/voir la Bretagne/jamais

   _____

2. Christophe/connaître/personne/l'été dernier

   _____

3. moi/travailler/nulle part

   _____

4. Olivier et Bernard/faire/rien/cette année

   _____

5. toi/voyager en Europe/pas encore

   _____

6. Luc/revoir Justine/plus

_____

7. ma famille/recevoir/personne

_____

8. mes copains/apprendre/rien

_____

9. nous/écrire/jamais/à nos amis

_____

10. vous/jouer/nulle part

_____

La Bretagne

La Bretagne, or Brittany, is a region in western France, occupying the large peninsula that protrudes into the Atlantic Ocean. La Bretagne was settled in the sixth century by refugees from Britain fleeing the Germanic invasions. These people spoke Breton, a Celtic language related to Welsh and Gaelic. Breton was once the major language of the area, but is now rarely heard. Efforts are now being made to preserve Breton as a spoken and written medium of communication.

C. Le dîner. Create conversations about preparing a dinner for friends. Each exchange will consist of a question in the **passé composé** using inversion and a negative answer, also in the **passé composé.** Make sure to use the correct form of the indefinite and partitive articles in the answer.

Modèle Jean-Pierre/acheter/jus ➤
—Jean-Pierre a-t-il acheté du jus?
—Non, il n'a pas acheté de jus.

1. ta mère/préparer/hors-d'œuvres

— _____

— _____

2. tu/acheter/viande

— _____

— _____

➤➤➤➤➤

3. Odile/apporter/eau minérale

— _____

— _____

4. Caroline et Lise/faire/gâteau

— _____

— _____

5. vous/chercher/légumes

— _____

— _____

6. Marc/acheter/thé

— _____

— _____

III. The *passé composé* with *être*

■ Some French verbs form the **passé composé** using **être** as the auxiliary verb instead of **avoir.** When the **passé composé** is formed with **être,** the past participle agrees in gender and number with the subject of the sentence. Here is the **passé composé** of **aller** *(to go).*

PASSÉ COMPOSÉ OF ALLER

je **suis** allé(e)	nous **sommes** allé(e)s
tu **es** allé(e)	vous **êtes** allé(e)(s)
il **est** allé	ils **sont** allés
elle **est** allée	elles **sont** allées
on **est** allé	

Here is a list of verbs that form the **passé composé** with **être.** Note that they express motion or a change of state.

Verbs conjugated with *être*

aller *to go* ➤ **je suis allé(e)**

arriver *to arrive* ➤ **je suis arrivé(e)**

descendre *to descend, to stay (in a hotel)* ➤ **je suis descendu(e)**

devenir *to become* ➤ **je suis devenu(e)**

entrer *to enter* ➤ **je suis entré(e)**

monter *to climb, to go up* ➤ **je suis monté(e)**

mourir *to die* ➤ **je suis mort(e)**

naître *to be born* ➤ **je suis né(e)**

partir *to leave* ➤ **je suis parti(e)**

rentrer *to return home* ➤ **je suis rentré(e)**

rester *to stay, to remain* ➤ **je suis resté(e)**

retourner *to return* ➤ **je suis retourné(e)**

sortir *to leave* ➤ **je suis sorti(e)**

tomber *to fall* ➤ **je suis tombé(e)**

venir *to come* ➤ **je suis venu(e)**

■ When these verbs have prefixes added they are also conjugated with **être** in the **passé composé.**

    redescendre ➤ je suis redescendu(e), **revenir** ➤ je suis revenue(e), etc.

D. Où sont-ils? It's the annual family gathering of the Rousseaus and there's no one around. Tell where they have all gone by forming sentences in the **passé composé** from the elements given.

1. Luc et Janine/sortir

    _____

2. Grand-mère/monter dans sa chambre

    _____

3. moi/descendre au sous-sol

    _____

4. le chat/rester dans le jardin

    _____

5. mes cousines/arriver en retard

    _____

6. la tante Marcelle/pas encore/venir

    _____

7. papa et mon oncle François/déjà/partir

    _____

➤➤➤➤➤

8. Philippe et Bernard/rentrer chez eux

_____

9. la petite Odile/tomber sur l'escalier

_____

10. les autres enfants/pas encore/entrer

_____

E. Pas encore. You want to find out if everyone has gone where he is supposed to. You find out that no one has gone yet. Create the exchanges on this topic from the elements given. Use **est-ce que** and **déjà** in the questions and **ne... pas encore** in the answers.

Modèle Marthe/sortir ➤
—Est-ce que Marthe est déjà sortie?
—Non, elle n'est pas encore sortie.

1. les voisins/partir en vacances

— _____

— _____

2. maman/retourner

— _____

— _____

3. Rachel et Karine/rentrer chez elles

— _____

— _____

4. Serge/venir

— _____

— _____

5. Anne/descendre faire les courses

— _____

— _____

6. les invités/arriver

—_____

—_____

IV. Agreement of the Past Participle with *avoir* Verbs

■ The past participle of verbs forming the **passé composé** with **avoir** agrees in gender and number with a direct object, *if the direct object precedes the verb.* In most cases, this occurs with a direct object pronoun or in a question.

—Tu as lu **les histoires?** *(f.)*	*Have you read **the stories**?*
—Non, je ne **les** ai pas encore lu**es.**	*No, I haven't read **them** yet.*
—Ces **sandwichs** sont très bons.	*These **sandwiches** are very good.*
—Ma mère **les** a fait**s.**	*My mother made **them**.*
—Quelle **histoire** avez-vous préfer**ée?**	*Which **story** did you prefer?*

■ Note that object pronouns in the **passé composé** precede the auxiliary verb. The negative particle **ne** precedes the object pronoun. There is *no* agreement with preceding indirect object pronouns.

—Tu as écrit à **ta sœur?**	*Did you write to **your sister**?*
—Non, je **lui** ai téléphoné.	*No, I phoned **her**.*

F. **Qu'est-ce qu'on en a fait?** Use the cues in parentheses to explain what has happened to each of these things. Write sentences in the **passé composé** that have object pronouns. Pay special attention to the agreement of the past participle.

Modèle —Où est la bicyclette de Pierre? *(vendre)*
➤ —Il l'a vendue.

1. —Où sont les cadeaux des enfants? *(ouvrir)*

—_____

2. —Où est le sandwich de Jacquot? *(manger)*

—_____

3. —Où est la lettre de Georgette? *(mettre à la poste)*

—_____

4. —Où sont les aspirines de Marguerite? *(prendre)*

—_____

➤➤➤➤➤

5. —Où est la composition de Joséphine? *(écrire)*

— _____

6. —Où est la nouvelle robe de Véra? *(mettre)*

— _____

7. —Où est le nom de l'étudiant? *(effacer)*

— _____

8. —Où est l'adresse de l'étudiant? *(effacer)*

— _____

9. —Où sont les petits cousins de Maurice? *(emmener au zoo)*

— _____

10. —Où sont les gants de Caroline? *(perdre)*

— _____

G. La petite Marcelle a peur. Little Marcelle had a scary experience. Retell it in the **passé composé.**

1. La petite Marcelle ne peut pas dormir.

_____

2. Elle descend du lit.

_____

3. Elle ouvre la porte de sa chambre.

_____

4. Elle regarde autour d'elle.

_____

5. Elle ne voit personne.

_____

6. Soudain, elle entend un bruit.

_____

7. Quelqu'un entre dans la cuisine!

_____

8. Elle n'a jamais tant de peur.

_____

9. Elle décide d'aller voir.

_____

10. Elle va vers l'escalier.

_____

11. Elle descend sans bruit.

_____

12. Elle pousse la porte de la cuisine.

_____

13. Elle l'ouvre lentement.

_____

14. Elle met la lumière.

_____

15. Qui voit-elle? Son chien!

_____

H. Questions personnelles. Answer the following questions in complete French sentences.

1. Qu'est-ce que vous avez fait ce week-end?

_____

2. Où est-ce que vous êtes allé l'été dernier?

_____

3. Quels devoirs avez-vous faits hier ou avant-hier?

_____

➤➤➤➤➤

4. Qu'est-ce qu'on vous a offert pour votre anniversaire?

_____

5. Qu'est-ce que vous avez mangé de bon cette semaine?

_____

I. **Composition.** Tell about what you did on your last vacation. Where did you go and with whom? What did you do? How long did you spend there?

The Imperfect;
Imperfect versus passé composé

I. The Imperfect

■ Like the **passé composé,** the imperfect refers to the past. But while the **passé composé** expresses completed actions, the imperfect is used in the following ways. (In the examples, the verbs in italics are in the imperfect.)

1. To provide background information, often setting the scene for an action or series of actions (in the **passé composé**)

   C'*était* une belle journée d'été. Il *faisait* beau et des nuages *flottaient* au ciel. Je *voulais* aller à la piscine donc j'ai téléphoné à mon amie Jackie.
   It was a beautiful summer day. The weather was nice and clouds were floating in the sky. I wanted to go to the pool, so I called my friend Jackie.

2. To describe an ongoing situation in the past *(was/were doing something),* sometimes interrupted by an event in the **passé composé**

   Nous *regardions* la télévision quand quelqu'un a sonné à la porte.
   We were watching TV when someone rang the doorbell.

3. To express repeated or habitual past actions *(used to do something)*

   Quand j'*étais* petit, nous *allions* presque tous les jours rendre visite à mes cousins. Ma tante nous *préparait* des petits gâteaux et nous les *mangions* dans le jardin.
   When I was little, we went (used to go) almost every day to visit my cousins. My aunt made cookies and we ate them in the garden.

■ The imperfect is formed by adding the endings -**ais**, -**ais**, -**ait**, -**ions**, -**iez**, -**aient** to the stem of the verb. The stem of the verb is the **nous** form of the present tense minus the -**ons** ending:

IMPERFECT OF PARLER (stem: **parl-**)

je parl**ais**	nous parl**ions**
tu parl**ais**	vous parl**iez**
il/elle/on parl**ait**	ils/elles parl**aient**

IMPERFECT OF FINIR (stem: **finiss-**)

je finiss**ais**	nous finiss**ions**
tu finiss**ais**	vous finiss**iez**
il/elle/on finiss**ait**	ils/elles finiss**aient**

IMPERFECT OF RENDRE (stem: **rend-**)

je rend**ais**	nous rend**ions**
tu rend**ais**	vous rend**iez**
il/elle/on rend**ait**	ils/elles rend**aient**

■ **-Er** verbs that have a spelling change in the **nous** form of the present tense (nous commençons, nous mangeons) have the same change in those forms of the imperfect where the ending begins with **a**: je commençais, je mangeais, ils commençaient, ils mangeaient but nous commencions, vous commenciez, nous mangions, vous mangiez.

Verbs whose stem ends in **i** have two **i**'s in the **nous** and **vous** forms of the imperfect: nous étudiions, vous étudiiez.

■ **Être** is the only verb that is irregular in the imperfect.

j'**étais**	nous **étions**
tu **étais**	vous **étiez**
il/elle/on **était**	ils/elles **étaient**

A. La jeunesse de Monsieur Garnier. Mr. Garnier, a 70-year-old man, is telling the two teenagers who live next door about his childhood. To find out what he says, create sentences from the elements given using the imperfect.

Modèle   ma famille/habiter la banlieue ➤ Ma famille habitait la banlieue.

1. nous/avoir un petit jardin

   _____

2. je/jouer dans le jardin avec mon chien

   _____

3. il/s'appeler «Soldat»

   _____

4. mon père/travailler en ville

   _____

5. ma mère/être à la maison avec moi et ma sœur

   _____

6. mes grands-parents/venir nous voir le dimanche

   _____

7. nous/manger tous ensemble

   _____

8. nous/être très heureux

   _____

B. Souvenirs de l'école primaire. A group of high school seniors is reminiscing about elementary school. Form sentences using the imperfect with each string of elements given to find out what each one says.

Modèle   RACHEL: nous/avoir/toujours/de bons professeurs
➤ Nous avions toujours de bons professeurs.

Des souvenirs

d'habitude *usually*

en général *in general*

la récréation *recess*

---

1. CORINNE: je/être/toujours/contente

   _____

2. ROBERT: mes petits copains/être/sympathiques

   _____

3. JEAN-MARC: tous les jours/je/manger/avec mes amis

   _____

4. ÉMILIE: nous/étudier/beaucoup

   _____

5. GÉRARD: tous les ans/je/connaître/beaucoup d'élèves

   _____

6. HÉLÈNE: d'habitude/je/sortir de chez moi/à huit heures moins vingt

   _____

7. CLAUDETTE: en général/les élèves/faire attention en classe

   _____

8. CHARLES: pendant la récréation/nous/jouer au football

   _____

C. Des activités parallèles. Pick elements from the two columns to form sentences telling what certain people were doing while other people were doing something else. Join the two parts of the sentence with the conjunction **pendant que** *(while)*. Create six sentences.

Modèle   Suzette + faire le linge / Corinne + écouter des compact-disques
> Suzette faisait le linge pendant que Corinne écoutait des compact-disques.

les personnes

Suzette
Marc et Louis
Corinne
les copains
Maman
Papa
les voisins
nous

les actions

finir ses/leurs devoirs
nettoyer sa/leur chambre
manger
préparer le dîner
ranger ses/leurs affaires
chercher son portefeuille
attendre dans la cuisine

rentrer
débarrasser la table
faire des haltères
dormir
écouter les informations
faire le café

La vie de tous les jours

le portefeuille *wallet*

débarrasser la table *to clear the table*

faire des haltères (le haltère) *to lift weights*

les informations *(fem. pl.) news*

---

1. _____

_____

2. _____

_____

3. _____

_____

4. _____

_____

5. _____

_____

6. _____

_____

D. Avant l'orage. Describe the changing scene before a storm. Use the imperfect of the verbs in parentheses. Remember that the imperfect is used for description of a scene in the past.

L'orage

au bord de *at the edge of, on the shore of*

baisser *to drop, diminish*

devenir *to become*

éclater *to burst, break, explode*

gronder *to rumble*

le lac *lake*

le nuage *cloud*

l'orage *(masc.) storm*

refroidir *to get colder or cooler*

le tonnerre *thunder*

Nous _____ (1. être) au bord du lac.

Il _____ (2. faire du vent). La température

_____ (3. baisser) et l'air _____ (4. refroidir).

Le ciel _____ (5. devenir) gris. Le tonnerre

_____ (6. gronder) au loin. Il _____

(7. y avoir) des nuages noirs à l'horizon. Un orage _____

(8. aller) éclater.

Le climat en France

France has four distinct climate zones:

- Central France and Eastern France (Paris, Lille, Nancy, Metz, Strasbourg) have a **continental climate.** In this area, summer is warm and winter cold, but with temperatures not reaching the extremes that they do in many parts of the United States.
- Western France—both the Atlantic coast and the areas on the English Channel (Normandy)—is in the **Atlantic climate** zone. The temperature is milder both in summer and winter than in the continental climate zone, but it rains a lot, as much as 240 days a year. This is a rich and fertile agricultural region.
- The mountainous areas of France (the Alps, the Pyrenees and the Massif Central) have what is called a **mountain climate**: a short summer and, in the higher elevations, a long and snowy winter.
- Tourists from northern Europe have always flocked to southern France for the **Mediterranean climate.** Here in Provence and Languedoc a short mild winter is followed by a long, hot, and dry summer, ideal for outdoor vacations.

II. *Si* + the Imperfect

■ **Si** followed by the **nous** form of the imperfect (or by the **on** form in colloquial speech) is used to make a suggestion or an invitation to do something.

Si nous fais*ions* une promenade en voiture?   *How about going for a ride?*

Si on sort*ait* tous ensemble?   *How about us all going out together?*

E. Des idées. Make suggestions to a friend to do the following things. Write each suggestion twice, once with **si** + the **nous** form of the imperfect, once with **si** + the **on** form of the imperfect.

Modèle   aller voir Jacqueline ➤ a. Si nous allions voir Jacqueline?
                                        b. Si on allait voir Jacqueline?

1. manger au restaurant

    a. _____

    b. _____

2. finir nos devoirs

    a. _____

    b. _____

3. ranger nos affaires

    a. _____

    b. _____

4. effacer le tableau

    a. _____

    b. _____

5. étudier à la bibliothèque

    a. _____

    b. _____

6. jouer aux échecs

    a. _____

    b. _____

III. Imperfect versus *passé composé*

■ As you have seen, there is no exact correspondence between the **passé composé** and imperfect in French and the English past. The **passé composé** is used for single, completed actions or for a *specified number* of completed actions. Certain words in a sentence are clues that the **passé composé** should be used: **une (deux, trois, …) fois** *(once, twice, three times, etc.)*; **soudain, tout à coup** *(suddenly);* **d'abord … puis … ensuite … enfin** *(first, then, then, finally);* time words, such as **hier, à trois heures, l'année dernière,** etc.

> **Nous sommes allés à Chamonix** *l'année dernière. D'abord,* **nous avons visité la ville,** *puis* **nous avons fait une promenade en montagne,** *enfin* **nous sommes rentrés à Paris.** *(specific events that occurred a single specified time)*
> *We went to Chamonix last year. First, we visited the town, then we hiked in the mountains, and finally we returned to Paris.*

■ Clue words for the imperfect, when it is used to express habitual or repeated past actions, are: **d'habitude, habituellement; toujours; souvent; le lundi, le mardi,** etc. *(on Mondays, on Tuesdays, etc.).*

> *Le dimanche,* **nous dinions chez Mémé.** *D'habitude* **elle préparait un énorme repas que nous prenions** *souvent* **dans la salle à manger sombre.** *(actions repeated an unspecified number of times)*
> *On Sundays, we used to have dinner at Grandmother's. She usually made a huge meal that we often ate in the somber dining room.*

■ Remember when telling what happened to use the imperfect to express the *background* for events. What actually happens (the action or change of state) is told in the **passé composé.** For instance, in the sentence

> **Il faisait beau quand je suis descendu.**   *The weather was nice when I went downstairs.*

Il faisait beau is the background against which the action **je suis descendu** takes place.

Descriptions of time and weather in the past are commonly expressed in the imperfect.

F. Quel temps faisait-il? Tell what the weather was like when each of these events took place during Sylvie's day.

Modèle   faire mauvais/je/sortir ➤ Il faisait mauvais quand je suis sortie.

1. faire du vent/je/voir Monique

_____

2. faire assez froid/nous/prendre l'autobus

_____

3. pleuvoir/nous/descendre de l'autobus

_____

4. faire mauvais/Claudette/nous voir

_____

5. neiger/nous/décider d'entrer dans un magasin de vêtements

_____

6. neiger fort/on/sortir du magasin

_____

G. Quelle heure était-il? Serge and his friends live in the Paris suburbs and are spending Saturday in Paris. Tell how they got to Paris by recounting their morning step by step, using the times given.

Modèle   7h30/mon réveil/sonner
➤ Il était sept heures et demie quand mon réveil a sonné.

1. 9h/Luc et Pierre/arriver

_____

2. 9h15/nous/sortir

_____

3. 9h30/mon père/nous déposer à la gare

_____

4. 9h40/le train/venir

_____

5. 10h30/nous/arriver à Paris

_____

H. Qu'est-ce qui se passait? Actions talked about in the imperfect can serve as backgrounds for other actions. Use the following grid to write sentences that have a background action and an event. The event will of course be in the **passé composé.**

Modèle

subject	background	subject	event
je	prendre mon petit déjeuner	je	recevoir un coup de téléphone de Maurice

➤ Je prenais mon petit déjeuner quand j'ai reçu un coup de téléphone de Maurice.

	subject	background	subject	event
1.	Luc	lire	ses amis	téléphoner
2.	Chrystelle	regarder la télé	Justine	venir la voir
3.	les enfants	jouer dans le jardin	il	commencer à pleuvoir
4.	Mme Savignon	faire ses courses	elle	rencontrer Mme Oudot
5.	M. Deschênes	laver la voiture	sa femme	rentrer du marché
6.	vous	prendre le goûter	nous	frapper à la porte
7.	Philippe	faire ses devoirs	il	entendre ses amis dans la rue
8.	le professeur	préparer sa leçon	les étudiants	ouvrir la porte

1. _____

   _____

2. _____

   _____

3. _____

   _____

4. _____

   _____

5. _____

   _____

6. _____

   _____

7. _____

   _____

8. _____

   _____

IV. Special Meanings of Certain Verbs

Some common verbs have different meanings in the imperfect and the **passé composé**:

- **vouloir**: imperfect *wanted to;* **passé composé** *tried to*

Il *voulait* rentrer.	He **wanted to** return home.
Il *a voulu* rentrer.	He **tried to** return home.

- **savoir**: imperfect *knew;* **passé composé** *found out*

Je *savais* son nom.	I **knew** her name.
J'*ai su* son nom.	I **found out** her name.

- **connaître**: imperfect *knew;* **passé composé** *met, made the acquaintance of*

Vous *connaissiez* nos amis?	**Did** you **know** our friends?
Vous *avez connu* nos amis?	**Did** you **meet** our friends?

- **pouvoir**: imperfect *could (but didn't necessarily);* **passé composé** *could (succeeded at)*

Nous *pouvions* le faire.	We **were able** to do it. (but didn't necessarily do it)
Nous *avons pu* le faire.	We **were able** to do it. (**and succeeded** at doing it)

- **avoir**: imperfect *had;* **passé composé** *got*

Elle *avait* une idée.	She **had** an idea.
Elle *a eu* une idée.	She **got** an idea.

I. **En français, s'il vous plaît.** Express the following exchanges in French, keeping in mind the special meanings of **vouloir, savoir, connaître, pouvoir,** and **avoir** in the **passé composé** and imperfect.

1. I didn't know her address.
   When did you *(tu)* find it out?

   — _____

   — _____

2. Didn't they want to come to the party? Why didn't they come?
   Yes, they wanted to, but they couldn't.

   — _____

   — _____

3. Did he know your *(fam.)* sister?
   Yes, he met her last week.

   — _____

   — _____

4. Were you *(tu)* hungry?
   Yes, I got hungry after the match.

   — _____

   — _____

J. **Composition.** Describe the last trip you took or vacation you went on. Make sure to describe not only the events of the trip (**passé composé**), but also the circumstances: the time, the weather, the background against which the events happened. Write a paragraph of six to eight sentences.

Commands (The Imperative)

I. Formation of Commands

- For almost all verbs in French, the commands are the same as the **tu** and **vous** forms of the present tense without the subject pronouns.

Écris à tes parents aujourd'hui.	*Write to your parents today.*
N'attends pas.	*Don't wait.*
Réfléchissez un peu. Ne **sortez** pas sous la pluie.	*Think about it a little. Don't go out in the rain.*

- In the **tu** commands of **-er** verbs, the final **s** of the present tense is dropped. The final **s** is also dropped in the familiar imperative of **aller** (**tu vas** ➢ **va!**) and of **-ir** verbs conjugated like **-er** verbs, such as **ouvrir** (**tu ouvres** ➢ **ouvre!**).

Travaille! Ne **joue** pas avec ton crayon.	*Work! Don't play with your pencil.*
Offre un cadeau à ton chef. **N'oublie** pas.	*Give a gift to your boss. Don't forget.*

- The **nous** form of verbs without the subject pronoun is the first person plural command. It is the equivalent of English *let's do something*.

Ne **restons** pas dans la rue. **Entrons** dans le café.	*Let's not stay in the street. Let's go into the café.*

- The verbs **avoir** and **être** have irregular imperative forms.

  avoir: **aie, ayons, ayez**

  être: **sois, soyons, soyez**

A. Le dîner. Marie and Christine are having friends over for dinner. What are they telling each other to do to get ready? Write the necessary familiar commands to find out.

Modèle *(prendre les assiettes)* ➤ Prends les assiettes.

À table	
couper *to cut*	**sortir** *to take out*
remplir *to fill*	**le saucisson** *salami*

1. *(mettre la table)* _____

2. *(choisir une cassette)* _____

3. *(remplir les verres)* _____

4. *(ne pas laisser la bouteille sur la table)* _____

   _____

5. *(ne pas sortir le gâteau)* _____

6. *(couper le saucisson)* _____

7. *(ne pas fermer les fenêtres)* _____

8. *(On sonne. Ouvrir la porte)* _____

B. Des conseils. Solange is giving some advice to her friend Pierre who is having trouble getting his schoolwork done. Find out what she tells him to do by writing out these phrases as familiar commands.

Modèle *(ne pas dormir jusqu'à dix heures)* ➤ Ne dors pas jusqu'à dix heures.

1. *(prendre ton petit déjeuner à sept heures)*

   _____

2. *(ne pas rester chez toi)*

   _____

3. *(aller à la bibliothèque)*

   _____

➤➤➤➤➤

4. *(trouver une place où tu peux être seul)*

_____

5. *(être patient)*

_____

6. *(commencer à étudier tout de suite)*

_____

7. *(ne pas chercher tes amis)*

_____

8. *(faire attention à ton travail)*

_____

C. Au bureau. The receptionist comes to take Mme Laurent to see Mlle Duval. She gives Mme Laurent instructions using the **vous** form of the imperative. Write out what she tells her.

Modèle *(prendre vos affaires)* ➤ Prenez vos affaires.

1. *(ne pas attendre ici)* _____

2. *(venir avec moi)* _____

3. *(pousser cette porte)* _____

4. *(prendre ce couloir)* _____

5. *(au fond, tourner à droite)* _____

6. *(aller à la troisième porte)* _____

7. *(frapper)* _____

8. *(entrer)* _____

D. Le pique-nique. Your friend proposes some ideas for a picnic. You respond either affirmatively or negatively, using the command forms for **nous.**

Modèles   Si on faisait un pique-nique? *(bonne idée)*
      ➤ Bonne idée. Faisons un pique-nique.

        Si on invitait Luc et Christine. *(non)*
      ➤ Non. N'invitons pas Luc et Christine.

Le pique-nique

la balle *ball*   **de bonne heure** *early*

la campagne *country(side)*   **le panier** *basket*

---

1. Si on allait à la campagne? *(bonne idée)*

   _____

2. Si on prenait le train? *(non)*

   _____

3. Si on partait de bonne heure? *(bonne idée)*

   _____

4. Si on apportait nos bicyclettes? *(non)*

   _____

5. Si on apportait une balle? *(bonne idée)*

   _____

6. Si on achetait de la limonade? *(non)*

   _____

7. Si on préparait des sandwichs? *(bonne idée)*

   _____

8. Si on remplissait nos paniers? *(non)*

   _____

E. Des indications. You're giving directions in a French city to someone who wants to find a doctor's office located at 78, rue Richelieu. To do that, turn each phrase into a sentence with a formal command.

Modèle   aller au coin ➤ Allez au coin.

Où se trouve...?

à gauche/droite *to the left/right*	**tout droit** *straight*
jusqu'au bout *until the end*	**traverser** *to cross*

---

1. prendre cette rue   _____

2. aller tout droit   _____

3. continuer jusqu'au bout   _____

4. tourner à gauche   _____

5. suivre la rue Richelieu jusqu'à la rue Louis XIV _____

    _____

6. traverser la rue Louis XIV   _____

7. chercher le numéro 78   _____

8. sonner et entrer   _____

Un peu d'histoire

Many French streets are named after famous historical figures.

■ **Le cardinal Richelieu,** a French statesman, was the dominant power in France under Louis XIII (1610–1643). A great reformer, he made important changes in the finances of the nation and in the army. He encouraged the development of a strong fleet of trading ships, and under his influence France took its first steps toward the creation of a colonial empire. He founded a company to colonize Canada and set up a French trading post in Madagascar.

■ **Louis XIV,** also known as **Le Roi Soleil,** was king of France from 1643–1715. Through warfare he enlarged the borders of France. He moved the royal court to Versailles, a small town 14 kilometers southwest of Paris, and had the lavish Palace of Versailles built. A spectacular building surrounded by magnificent French-style formal gardens, Versailles attracts millions of visitors every year. Under Louis XIV, French art, music, and literature flourished, and the French classical theater was born. The most famous playwrights of the period are Corneille, Racine, and Molière.

II. Object Pronouns with Commands

■ In affirmative commands, object pronouns follow the verb and are joined to it with a hyphen. The pronoun **me** becomes **moi** when it follows a command form.

—Dis-**moi** si tu vas au cinéma.	*Tell **me** if you're going to the movies.*
—Luc veut voir le film.	*Luc wants to see the film too.*
Téléphone-**lui**.	*Call **him.***
—Et nos devoirs?	*And our homework?*
—Finissons-**les** demain.	*Let's finish **it** tomorrow.*

■ The final **s** of the **tu** form that is dropped in the imperative is restored (and pronounced as a **z** in liaison) before the pronouns **y** and **en** in affirmative **tu** commands.

Va au cinéma. ➢ **Vas-y.**   *Go to the movies. **Go there.***

Mange de la salade. ➢ **Manges-en.**   *Eat some salad. **Eat some.***

■ If two object pronouns follow an affirmative command, their order is different from the order of double object pronouns before the verb in statements.

	me (= moi)			
le	te (= toi)			
la before	lui	before y before	en
les	nous			
	vous			
	leur			

Moi shortens to **m'** before **en**: **m'en.**

—Tu as besoin de tes **logiciels**?	*Do you need your **software programs**?*
—Oui, rends-**les-moi**.	*Yes, give **them** back **to me.***
—Les enfants veulent apprendre **ce jeu**?	*Do the children want to learn **this game**?*
—Oui, enseignons-**le-leur**.	*Yes, let's teach **it** to **them.***
—Voulez-vous **du jus**?	*Do you want **some juice**?*
—Oui, servez-**m'en**, s'il vous plaît.	*Yes, serve **me some**, please.*

F. **Mais fais-le.** Françoise is unsure about what she should do. Her friend Janine tells her to do these things. Use the **tu** form of the imperative and the appropriate object pronoun to see what Janine says.

Modèle   —Je ne sais pas si je dois téléphoner *à Guillaume.*
     ➢ —Mais oui. Téléphone-lui.

1. —Je ne sais pas si je dois vendre *ma chaîne-stéréo.*

   — _____

2. —Je ne sais pas si je dois aller *au parc.*

   — _____

➢➢➢➢➢

3. —Je ne sais pas si je dois prendre *les billets.*

   —_____

4. —Je ne sais pas si je dois acheter *des bonbons.*

   —_____

5. —Je ne sais pas si je dois écrire *à mes cousins.*

   —_____

6. —Je ne sais pas si je dois apporter *des fleurs.*

   —_____

7. —Je ne sais pas si je dois répondre *à Carole.*

   —_____

8. —Je ne sais pas si je dois rester *dans le restaurant.*

   —_____

G. Qu'est-ce qu'il faut faire? Marc is asking his friend Annette for advice. Phrase her replies as **tu** commands and replace object nouns in italics by the appropriate pronouns.

Modèles   Est-ce qu'il faut rendre *ce livre à Maurice? (oui)*
     ➤ Oui, rends-le-lui.

           Est-ce qu'il faut dire *ce secret à Lise? (non)*
     ➤ Non, ne le lui dis pas.

1. Est-ce qu'il faut montrer *la rédaction au professeur? (non)*

   _____

2. Est-ce qu'il faut donner *des bonbons aux enfants? (oui)*

   _____

3. Est-ce qu'il faut servir *ce poisson à nos invités? (non)*

   _____

4. Est-ce qu'il faut apporter *ce journal à M. Fontanet? (oui)*

   _____

5. Est-ce qu'il faut envoyer *ce cadeau à Marthe? (non)*

   _____

6. Est-ce qu'il faut demander *de l'argent à mes parents?* (oui)

   _____

7. Est-ce qu'il faut prêter *ma bicyclette à Suzanne?* (non)

   _____

8. Est-ce qu'il faut expliquer *ces problèmes aux étudiants?* (oui)

   _____

H. Après avoir couru les magasins. Karine and Georgette have just come back from shopping and are looking over the things they bought. Use the verbs in parentheses as **nous** commands to see what suggestions they make. Replace all nouns in italics by object pronouns.

Modèles   Nous avons tant de *paquets! (ouvrir)* ➤ Ouvrons-les.

Voici *nos nouveaux chemisiers. (ne pas/essayer)* ➤ Ne les essayons pas.

Le shopping
échanger *to exchange*   **pendre** *to hang up*
le foulard *silk scarf*

1. Ces *gants* sont trop petits. *(échanger)*

   _____

2. Les *paquets* sont un peu partout. *(ranger)*

   _____

3. Il nous faut encore *des foulards. (acheter)*

   _____

4. On peut rentrer *au magasin. (ne pas/aller)*

   _____

5. *Le vendeur* travaille encore. *(ne pas/téléphoner)*

   _____

6. On ne doit pas laisser *les nouveaux vêtements* sur le sofa. *(pendre)*

   _____

I. La première classe. The twins are nervous about their first day at school. Write what their mother says to calm them down using **vous** commands and replacing italicized nouns by object pronouns.

Modèles —Si *le professeur* est dans la classe quand on entre? *(saluer)*
➤ —Saluez-le.

—Il faut apporter *nos nouveaux cahiers*. *(ne pas/oublier)*
➤ Ne les oubliez pas.

1. Et si le prof nous pose *des questions*? *(répondre)* _____

2. Et si *notre voisin* essaie de nous parler pendant la leçon? *(ne pas/faire attention)*

   _____

3. Et si *le prof* veut voir *nos cahiers*? *(montrer)* _____

4. Et si le prof nous donne *des devoirs*? *(noter)* _____

5. Et s'il nous faut écrire *un paragraphe*? *(finir)* _____

6. Et si *le professeur* est très sévère? *(ne pas/avoir peur)*

   _____

J. Composition. Write out one of the following scenes using as many command forms and object pronouns as possible.

1. A father is giving his daughter advice about looking for a summer job.

2. A storekeeper is telling his staff what to do to get ready to open the store.

3. Two friends are making suggestions to each other about what they might do this weekend.

Reflexive Verbs

I. Formation of Reflexive Verbs

■ Reflexive verbs are always conjugated with a reflexive pronoun. A reflexive pronoun always refers to the same person or thing that is the subject.

SE LAVER *(TO WASH UP)*

je **me** lave *I wash*	nous **nous** lavons *we wash*
tu **te** laves *you wash*	vous **vous** lavez *you wash*
il/elle/on **se** lave *he/she washes*	ils/elles **se** lavent *people/they/we wash*
on **se** lave *it washes*	

The reflexive pronoun precedes the conjugated verb form. When a reflexive verb is made negative, the word **ne** precedes the reflexive pronoun and **pas** follows the verb.

—Tu **te réveilles** toujours de bonne heure?

Do you always get up early?

—Non, le dimanche je **ne** me lève **pas** avant onze heures.

No, on Sundays I don't get up before eleven o'clock.

La routine

se brosser les cheveux, les dents *to brush one's hair, teeth*

se coucher *to go to bed*

se déshabiller *to get undressed*

s'endormir *to fall asleep*

s'habiller *to get dressed*

se laver les mains, la figure, la tête *to wash one's hands, one's face, one's hair*

se lever *to get up*

se maquiller *to put on makeup*

se peigner *to comb one's hair*

se raser *to shave*

se reposer *to rest*

se réveiller *to wake up*

A. La journée de Philippe. Philippe describes a typical day of his. Write out what he says using the verbs and expressions given.

Modèle se réveiller/6h30
> ➤ Je me réveille à six heures et demie.

1. se lever/tout de suite

    _____

2. se brosser les dents/d'abord

    _____

3. se laver/après

    _____

4. se raser/tous les jours

    _____

5. s'habiller/immédiatement

    _____

6. se peigner/avant de descendre

    _____

7. se coucher/à onze heures du soir

    _____

8. s'endormir/tout de suite

    _____

B. On demande. Marie wants to know why people are not doing what you would expect given the circumstances. Write out her questions using the reflexive verbs given.

Modèle Jacques a son premier cours à huit heures. *(se lever)*
➤ —Pourquoi est-ce qu'il ne se lève pas alors?

On se déplace

s'approcher de *to approach*

s'asseoir *to sit down*

se dépêcher *to hurry up*

se déplacer *to move, to move around, to travel*

s'éloigner de *to move away from*

s'installer *to move in, settle in*

se mettre en route *to get going, to start out*

se promener *to take a walk*

se retrouver *to meet (by appointment)*

1. Les enfants sont fatigués. *(se coucher)*

   _____

2. Je dois sortir. *(s'habiller)*

   _____

3. Martine a les cheveux mouillés. *(se sécher les cheveux)*

   _____

4. Le bébé pleure. *(s'endormir)*

   _____

5. Luc et moi, on est pressés. *(se dépêcher)*

   _____

6. Christine n'entend pas bien le professeur. *(s'approcher)*

   _____

7. Toi et moi, nous devons faire de l'exercice. *(se promener)*

   _____

8. Jacques veut arriver à Marseille avant minuit. *(se mettre en route)*

   _____

II. The Infinitive of Reflexive Verbs

- If the reflexive verb is used in the infinitive, the reflexive pronoun precedes the infinitive and agrees with the subject.

—Tu vas **te fatiguer** si tu continues comme ça.   *You're going **to get tired** if you keep on like that.*

—Tu as raison. Je dois **me reposer.**   *You're right. I ought **to rest.***

- The negative of verb + infinitive constructions is formed by placing **ne** before the conjugated verb and **pas** after it, *before* the reflexive pronoun.

—Nous **n'**allons **pas nous** amuser là-bas.   *We're **not** going to have a good time there.*

—Vous **ne** devez **pas vous** plaindre tout le temps.   *You should**n't** complain all the time.*

C. De bons conseils. Write Martin's suggestions about people using **devoir** + the infinitive given.

Les émotions, les réactions et les sentiments

s'amuser *to have a good time*

s'animer *to perk up, feel more lively*

se calmer *to calm down*

se détendre *to relax*

s'embêter *to get/be bored (colloquial)*

s'ennuyer *to get/be bored*

se fâcher *to get angry*

se fatiguer *to get tired*

s'impatienter *to get impatient*

s'inquiéter *to worry*

s'intéresser *to be interested in*

se mettre en colère *to get angry*

s'offenser *to get insulted, offended*

se passionner (**pour**) *to get excited (about)*

se plaindre (**de**) *to complain (about)*

se sentir *to feel*

Modèle   Philippe est très nerveux. *(devoir/se calmer)*
    ➤ Il doit se calmer.

1. Odile et Sandrine sont furieuses. *(ne pas devoir/se mettre en colère)*

   _____

2. Frédéric est découragé. *(devoir/s'animer)*

   _____

3. Je suis très, très pressé. *(ne pas devoir/s'impatienter)*

   _____

4. Danielle et moi, nous sommes très inquiets. *(ne pas devoir/s'inquiéter)*

   _____

5. Tu as l'air très fatigué. *(devoir/se détendre)*

   _____

6. Toi et Paulette, vous allez être en retard. *(devoir/se mettre en route)*

   _____

D. Devinons les réactions. A brother and sister are discussing how people might react if they do certain things. Use **aller** + the infinitive given to find out what they think.

Modèle   Qu'est-ce qui va arriver si nous ne mangeons pas le gâteau
           de grand-mère? *(s'offenser)*
           ➤ Elle va s'offenser.

1. Que va dire maman si je rentre à une heure du matin? *(s'inquiéter)*

   _____

2. Et si papa voit que j'ai eu une mauvaise note en chimie? *(se fâcher)*

   _____

3. Que va dire le prof si je n'étudie pas? *(s'impatienter)*

   _____

4. Qu'est-ce qui va arriver si ton petit ami oublie ton anniversaire?
   (se mettre en colère)

   _____

5. Comment va réagir notre petit frère si on l'emmène au concert? *(s'embêter)*

   _____

6. Et si on l'emmène au match de football? *(s'amuser)*

   _____

E. Une journée très mouvementée. Antoinette's whole family is rushing to get ready today. Write sentences with the verb + infinitive construction that tell what is going on.

Modèle   nous/vouloir/se mettre en route à dix heures
➤ Nous voulons nous mettre en route à dix heures.

1. grand-père/aller/faire le café

   _____

2. moi/devoir/s'habiller tout de suite

   _____

3. mes frères/aller/s'impatienter

   _____

4. ma petite sœur/ne pas vouloir/se lever

   _____

5. maman/aller/se peigner

   _____

6. nous/ne pas pouvoir/se détendre

   _____

7. ma sœur et moi/devoir/s'installer dans la cuisine

   _____

8. tout le monde/aller/se dépêcher

   _____

III. Reflexive Verbs in the *passé composé*

■ Reflexive verbs are conjugated with **être** in the **passé composé.** The reflexive pronoun comes right before the form of **être.** In most cases, the past participle agrees in gender and number with the reflexive pronoun.

PASSÉ COMPOSÉ OF SE LAVER *(TO WASH UP)*

je me **suis** lavé(e)	nous nous **sommes** lavé(e)s
tu t'**es** lavé(e)	vous vous **êtes** lavé(e)(s)
il s'**est** lavé	ils se **sont** lavés
elle s'**est** lavée	elles se **sont** lavées
on s'**est** lavé(e)	

■ Sometimes a reflexive verb has a direct object following it, as in **se laver la tête** (*to wash one's hair*). In these phrases the past participle does *not* agree with the reflexive pronoun in the **passé composé.**

PASSÉ COMPOSÉ OF SE LAVER LA TÊTE
(TO WASH ONE'S HAIR)

je me suis lav**é** la tête	nous nous sommes lav**é** la tête
tu t'es lav**é** la tête	vous vous êtes lav**é** la tête
il s'est lav**é** la tête	ils se sont lav**é** la tête
elle s'est lav**é** la tête	elles se sont lav**é** la tête
on s'est lav**é** la tête	

■ In the negative of reflexive verbs in the **passé composé, ne** precedes the reflexive pronoun and **pas** comes between **être** and the past participle.

Ils **ne** se sont **pas** levés à temps et ils **ne** se sont **pas** mis en route.   *They didn't get up on time and they didn't get going on their trip.*

F. **On ne bouge pas.** Mother is checking with her daughter to see if everyone is getting ready on time this morning. Create conversations in which the daughter informs her mother that no one has yet done what he or she is supposed to do.

Modèle   ton père/s'habiller ➤
—Est-ce que ton père s'est déjà habillé?
—Non, il ne s'est pas encore habillé.

1. Christine et Janine/se lever

— _____

— _____

2. grand-mère/s'asseoir dans la cuisine

— _____

— _____

3. toi/se laver

— _____

— _____

4. ta tante/se mettre en route

— _____

— _____

➤➤➤➤➤

5. ta sœur/se maquiller

— _____

— _____

6. la petite Monique/se brosser les dents

— _____

— _____

7. les enfants/se laver les mains

— _____

— _____

IV. Reciprocal Reflexives

■ The plural reflexive pronouns (**nous, vous, se**) can also be used to express reciprocal actions *(each other)*.

Maurice et Carole **se voient** tous les jours.

*Maurice and Carole see **each other** every day.*

■ In many reciprocal verbs, the reflexive pronoun is an indirect object, and therefore there is no agreement of the past participle in the **passé composé**. You can tell which reflexive pronouns are indirect objects by looking at the corresponding non-reflexive verb. For instance, **parler** takes an indirect object (Je **lui** parle. *I speak to her.*) so the reflexive pronoun in **se parler** *(to speak to each other)* is an indirect object. There is *no* agreement of the past participle: **ils se sont parlé.**

Des verbes réciproques

s'aimer *to like, to love each other*

se connaître *to know, to meet each other*

In the following verbs the reflexive pronoun is an indirect object.

se donner rendez-vous *to make an appointment to see each other*

se parler *to speak to each other*

se téléphoner *to telephone each other*

se voir *to see each other*

G. Une journée au Louvre. Three friends have decided to spend the day in the Louvre Museum in Paris and go to the movies in the evening. Form sentences in the **passé composé** from each string of elements to find out what their day was like.

Projets

se charger de *to take care of, to take charge of*

s'en aller *to go away, to leave*

s'occuper de *to take care of, to take charge of*

se quitter *to leave each other*

se réunir *to get together*

Modèle   les trois amis/se lever/de bonne heure
➤ Les trois amis se sont levés de bonne heure.

1. ils/se téléphoner

   _____

2. ils/se donner rendez-vous devant le Louvre

   _____

3. ces trois amis/se connaître au lycée

   _____

4. Alice/se charger des billets de cinéma

   _____

5. Robert/s'occuper du déjeuner

   _____

6. ils/se réunir à dix heures

   _____

7. après la visite du Louvre, ils/se promener

   _____

8. ils/s'amuser au cinéma

   _____

➤➤➤➤➤

9. ils/se quitter à minuit

_____

10. ils/ne pas/s'ennuyer ensemble

_____

Le Louvre

The **Louvre** Museum on the right bank of the Seine River houses one of the world's greatest collections of artistic treasures. The Louvre was originally the palace of the French kings. The art collections of the Louvre are outstanding not only in painting (the _Mona Lisa_ by Leonardo Da Vinci) but also in the art of the ancient world. You can see the column carved with Hammurabi's laws, the jewels of the Pharaoh Ramses II, and the Venus de Milo. The entrance to the Louvre is now marked by a much discussed modernistic glass pyramid that contrasts with the Renaissance style building.

V. The Imperative of Reflexive Verbs

■ In affirmative commands with reflexive verbs, the reflexive pronoun follows the verb and is attached to it by a hyphen. The reflexive pronoun **te** becomes **toi** in affirmative commands.

Brosse-**toi** les dents.	_Brush your teeth._
Dépêchons-**nous**.	_Let's hurry up._
Levez-**vous**.	_Get up._

■ In negative commands, the reflexive pronoun is in its usual position before the verb. **Te** does not change to **toi** in negative commands.

Ne **te** fâche pas.	_Don't get angry._
Ne **nous** asseyons pas.	_Let's not sit down._
Ne **vous** inquiétez pas.	_Don't worry._

H. Gentil moniteur. You're a camp counselor. What imperatives would you use to set some rules for your group? Give the commands you would need in two ways, first directed to one camper and then to the entire group.

Modèle   se lever ➤ _À un enfant:_ Lève-toi.
                            Au groupe: Levez-vous.

Les enfants

se battre _to fight_	**se perdre** _to get lost_
se disputer _to argue_	**se servir de** _to use_

	À un enfant	Au groupe d'enfants
1. se coucher tôt	_____	_____
2. se réveiller tôt	_____	_____
3. s'habiller vite	_____	_____
4. se peigner tous les jours	_____	_____
5. ne pas se battre	_____	_____
6. ne pas se disputer	_____	_____
7. s'amuser	_____	_____
8. ne pas se perdre	_____	_____

I. **Questions personnelles.** Answer the following questions in complete French sentences.

1. Quand est-ce que vous vous fâchez?

   _____

2. Avec qui est-ce que vous vous disputez souvent?

   _____

3. Dans quelles situations est-ce que vous vous ennuyez?

   _____

4. Quand est-ce que vous vous inquiétez?

   _____

5. Est-ce que vous et vos amis vous téléphonez souvent? Expliquez.

   _____

J. **Composition.** Describe a typical school day for you—your routine, your time in school or work, your getting together with friends. Use as many reflexive verbs as possible and describe your reactions as well as what happened.

Relative Clauses

I. Relative Clauses; the Relative Pronoun *qui*

■ A dependent clause is a part of a sentence that has its own subject and verb but cannot stand by itself: the girl *who goes to school with me* is sick today. Relative (dependent) clauses describe nouns much in the same way that adjectives do. Relative clauses in French begin with a relative pronoun such as **qui** or **que.**

l'étudiant **travailleur**	*the **hard-working** student*
l'étudiant **qui étudie beaucoup**	*the student **who studies a lot***

■ The relative pronoun **qui** in French refers both to people and things. **Qui** is always the subject of the relative clause.

le livre **qui** est sur la table	*the book **which** is on the table*
les passagers **qui** ont déjà pris leurs billets	*the passengers **who** have already bought their tickets*

■ When a relative clause beginning with **qui** has a verb in the **passé composé** conjugated with **être,** the past participle agrees with **qui. Qui** has the gender and number of the noun it refers to, its antecedent.

les trains **qui** sont partis	*the trains **that** left*
les jeunes filles **qui** sont arriv**ées** en avance	*the girls **who** arrived early*

■ **Qui** also determines the agreement of reflexive verbs in the **passé composé** since the reflexive pronoun refers back to it.

les familles **qui** se sont mis**es** en route	*the families **that** set out*

A. Précisons. Specify which person or thing is meant by turning each characteristic into a relative clause beginning with **qui.**

Modèle   Quel médecin? (Il a un cabinet dans l'immeuble d'en face.)
➤ Le médecin **qui** a un cabinet dans l'immeuble d'en face.

1. Quel restaurant?

   a. Il est sur la place. _____

   b. Il est ouvert tous les jours. _____

   c. Il a des prix très raisonnables. _____

2. Quels enfants?

    a. Ils jouaient au football. _____

    b. Ils sont tombés. _____

    c. Ils se sont disputés. _____

3. Quelle musicienne?

    a. Elle joue de la flûte. _____

    b. Elle a beaucoup de talent. _____

    c. Elle enseigne au conservatoire. _____

4. Quelles voitures?

    a. Elles vont vite. _____

    b. Elles coûtent cher. _____

    c. Elles consomment peu d'essence. _____

B. Mon lycée. Marie-Christine is describing her secondary school to an American friend. Combine each pair of sentences into a single one using the relative pronoun **qui** to find out what she says.

Modèle   Je vais au lycée. Mon lycée est dans ce quartier.
         ➤ Je vais au lycée qui est dans ce quartier.

1. J'ai beaucoup de copains. Mes copains sont très sympathiques.

    _____

2. Je suis des cours. Mes cours sont très intéressants.

    _____

3. J'ai des professeurs. Mes professeurs sont excellents.

    _____

4. Il y a un terrain de sport. Le terrain de sport est derrière le lycée.

    _____

5. Il y a beaucoup d'étudiants. Ces étudiants font du sport.

    _____

6. On nous donne beaucoup de devoirs. Les devoirs sont parfois très difficiles.

    _____

➢➢➢➢➢

7. Je déjeune à la cantine. La cantine est toujours plein de monde.

_____

8. Il y a des salades. Les salades sont délicieuses.

_____

II. The Relative Pronoun *que*

■ The relative pronoun **que** in French refers both to people and things. **Que** is always the object of the verb of the relative clause.

la chanteuse **que** j'ai écouté	*the singer **whom** I heard*
l'appartement **que** nous voulons louer	*the apartment **that** we want to rent*

■ When a relative clause beginning with **que** has a verb in the **passé composé** conjugated with **avoir,** the past participle agrees with **que,** which is a preceding direct object. **Que** has the gender and number of its antecedent. Note that **que** is never left out in French as *that* or *whom* can be in English.

la robe **qu'**elle a mise	*the dress (**that**) she put on*
les étudiantes **que** nous avons connu**es**	*the (female) students (**whom**) we met*
les projets **que** j'ai faits	*the plans (**that**) I have made*

■ **Que** becomes **qu'** before a vowel.

les livres **qu'**elle a lus	*the books (**that**) she read*

C. **Lequel exactement?** Specify which person or thing is meant by turning each characteristic into a relative clause beginning with **que.**

Modèle   Quels jeunes gens? (Nous **les** avons connus il y a un an.)
➤ Les jeunes gens que nous avons connus il y a un an.

1. Quels vêtements?

a. Nous les avons achetés. _____

b. Tu les as essayés. _____

c. Nous les avons mis dans la penderie.

_____

2. Quelle matière?

a. Je l'enseigne. _____

b. Vous l'aimez. _____

c. Tout le monde veux l'étudier. _____

3. Quelles femmes d'affaires?

    a. Nous les connaissons.   _____

    b. Vous les admirez.   _____

    c. Je les ai emmenés à la gare.   _____

4. Quel garçon?

    a. Nous l'avons invité.   _____

    b. Tu l'as vu hier.   _____

    c. Le prof le cherche.   _____

D. La musique. Jean-Christophe is talking about his taste in music. Combine each pair of sentences into a single one using the relative pronoun **que** to find out what he says.

Modèle   Ce sont les chansons folkloriques. J'aime les chansons folkloriques le plus.
      ➢ Ce sont les chansons folkloriques que j'aime le plus.

1. Il y a des chanteurs. J'adore ces chanteurs.

   _____

2. Je vais te montrer les compact-disques. J'ai acheté les compact-disques.

   _____

3. Voici un compact-disque. Je n'ai pas encore ouvert ce compact-disque.

   _____

4. Ce disque a des chansons. J'ai appris ces chansons par cœur.

   _____

5. Il y a aussi des symphonies. J'aime les symphonies.

   _____

6. Brahms est le compositeur. J'admire Brahms le plus.

   _____

7. À la radio il y a des concerts. J'écoute ces concerts le samedi.

   _____

8. Il y a aussi des concerts à la télé. Je regarde ces concerts.

   _____

E. **La nouvelle maison.** Jacques is showing his friend Olivier pictures of his new house in Alsace, on the outskirts of the city of Strasbourg. Complete his narration by adding either **qui** or **que**.

1. Voici la maison _____ nous avons achetée.

2. C'est une maison _____ est plus grande que notre appartement actuelle.

3. Je vais te montrer la chambre _____ j'ai choisie.

4. La maison se trouve dans une rue _____ est très tranquille.

5. C'est une maison _____ on a construite en 1980.

6. Il y a un jardin _____ est très joli.

7. C'est ma mère _____ va s'occuper du jardin.

8. Strasbourg est une ville _____ nous plaît beaucoup.

L'Alsace

- The region of **Alsace** is in northeastern France, at the German border. The influence of German culture is evident in the region's architecture and traditions; the local dialects of the area are Germanic, but the official language is French. Strasbourg, the capital city, is an important economic, scientific, and cultural center and the seat of many institutions of the European community, such as the European Parliament.
- Historically, Alsace, and its neighboring region **La Lorraine,** have been sources of conflict between France and Germany. Alsace and part of Lorraine were ceded to Germany by France after the French defeat in the Franco-Prussian War (1870–1871); restored to France after the Allied victory in World War I (1914–1918); annexed by Germany after the defeat of France in 1940 (World War II); and restored to France after the Allied victory in Europe (May, 1945).
- Alsatian cooking has much in common with German cuisine. Its most famous dish, la **choucroute alsacienne,** consisting of sausages on a bed of sauerkraut, is typical of the style of cooking of the French **brasseries.**

F. Un rhume. Élisabeth has a bad cold. Find out what she's doing about it by completing her narration with **qui** and **que,** as required.

> ### La santé
>
> **agir** *to work (of medicine)*   **ordonner** *to prescribe*
>
> **conseiller** *to recommend*   **le sirop pour la toux** *cough syrup*
>
> **embêtant** *annoying (colloq.)*
>
> **exécuter une ordonnance** *to fill*
>   *a prescription*

1. J'ai un rhume _____ est très embêtant.

2. Je suis allée voir un médecin _____ mon voisin m'a recommandé.

3. Maintenant je prends les pillules _____ ce médecin m'a ordonnées.

4. Il m'a conseillé un sirop pour la toux _____ je prends trois fois par jour.

5. C'est un sirop _____ me fait beaucoup de bien.

6. Il m'a donné des médicaments _____ agissent vite.

7. Il y a une pharmacie près de chez moi _____ exécute les ordonnances.

8. Je prends aussi des vitamines _____ sont bonnes pour la santé.

G. Les affaires de Raoul. Raoul is looking for some things he misplaced. Express them in French, making sure to include the necessary relative pronouns.

1. the book he read   _____

2. the backpack he lost   _____

3. the money he found   _____

4. the pen he borrowed   _____

5. the notes he lent   _____

6. the composition he wrote   _____

7. the ski jacket he was wearing   _____

8. the homework he finished   _____

III. The Relative Pronouns *ce qui* and *ce que*

■ The relative pronouns **ce qui** and **ce que** mean *what*. **Ce qui** is the subject of the verb in the relative clause, **ce que** is the object.

—Tu vois **ce qui** est sur la table?   *Do you see **what**'s on the table?*

—Je ne comprends pas **ce que** tu   *I don't understand **what** you mean.*
veux dire.

■ Do not confuse **ce qui** and **ce que** with the interrogatives **qu'est-ce qui** and **qu'est-ce que** which are used in questions. Remember that **qu'est-ce que** becomes **qu'est-ce qu'** and **ce que** becomes **ce qu'** before a vowel.

—**Qu'est-ce qui** les embête?   ***What** annoys them?*
—Je ne sais pas **ce qui** les embête.   *I don't know **what** annoys them.*

—**Qu'est-ce qu'**elle dit?   ***What** is she saying?*
—Je n'entends pas **ce qu'**elle dit.   *I don't hear **what** she's saying.*

■ **Ce qui** and **ce que** are used after **tout** to mean *all that, everything that*.

—Il faut savoir par cœur **tout ce**   *You have to know **everything that** is*
qui est dans ces notes.   *in these notes by heart.*

H. À compléter. Complete these sentences with **ce qui, ce que (ce qu')**, **Qu'est-ce qui**, or **Qu'est-ce que (Qu'est-ce qu')**, as appropriate. These sentences all have to do with school and assignments.

1. Apprenez-vous tout _____ est important pour l'examen?

2. _____ vous étudiez en ce moment?

3. Est-ce que je peux te demander _____ tu en penses?

4. Nous devons poser des questions aux étudiants. Il faut vérifier

   _____ les intéresse.

5. Je ne sais pas _____ il faut étudier pour demain.

6. Lève la main si tu ne comprends pas _____ le professeur dit.

7. _____ est essentiel dans ce livre?

8. _____ les élèves écrivent dans leurs cahiers?

9. Est-ce que tu aimes tout _____ on sert à la cantine?

10. J'ai perdu tout _____ était dans mon sac à dos.

I. **L'incompréhension.** Continue each of these sentences with another sentence that tells that the person mentioned hasn't a clue about what's going on. Your sentences will require either **ce qui** or **ce que.**

Modèle Il veut quelque chose. *(je ne sais pas)* ➤ Je ne sais pas ce qu'il veut.

1. Le professeur dit quelque chose. *(nous n'entendons pas)*

   _____

2. Quelque chose ennuie les étudiants. *(nous ne pouvons pas vérifier)*

   _____

3. Il a acheté quelque chose. *(il ne nous a pas dit)*

   _____

4. Elles cherchent quelque chose. *(nous ne savons pas)*

   _____

5. Quelque chose est sur le mur. *(je ne vois pas)*

   _____

6. Tu veux dire quelque chose. *(nous ne comprenons pas)*

   _____

7. Nous avons perdu quelque chose. *(vous ne savez pas)*

   _____

8. Quelque chose leur plaît. *(je ne sais pas)*

   _____

J. **Questions personnelles.** Answer each of the following sentences in a complete sentence containing a relative clause.

1. Quelle sorte de livres lisez-vous?

   _____

2. Quelle sorte de films allez-vous voir le plus souvent?

   _____

3. Quelle sorte de professeurs avez-vous cette année?

   _____

➤➤➤➤➤

4. Comment est votre appartement ou maison?

   _____

5. Quelle sorte d'émissions regardez-vous à la télé?

   _____

K. Composition. Pretend you are showing a friend around your town or around the place where you go on vacation. Describe the place using as many relative clauses as possible in sentences such as **Voilà le X qui/que...,** **Là-bas il y a des Y qui/que...,** etc. Write a paragraph of eight to ten sentences.

Adverbs

I. Adverbs

- Adverbs are words that modify verbs, adjectives, or other adverbs. Adverbs tell *when, where,* or *how* (in what manner). Both single words and phrases function as adverbs.

A. Trouvez les adverbes. Look at the following sentences and underline the adverbs or adverbial phrases.

1. Marie-Laure chante bien.

2. Vous parlez trop.

3. Les enfants sont très heureux.

4. Il commence à travailler à trois heures.

5. Nous restons ici.

6. Elle descend bientôt.

7. Les étudiants écoutent attentivement le professeur.

8. Je vois la ferme là-bas.

II. Adverbs of Time

- Here is a list of some common adverbs and adverbial phrases of time. Note that some of them, such as **après** and **avant,** can also function as prepositions when followed directly by a noun: **après la classe, avant le match.** These prepositional phrases usually function as adverbs.

après-demain *the day after tomorrow*	**encore une fois** *again*
autrefois *formerly, in the past*	**enfin** *at last, finally*
avant *before, previously, beforehand*	**longtemps** *for a long time*
avant-hier *the day before yesterday*	**quelquefois** *sometimes*
bientôt *soon*	**rarement** *seldom*
d'abord *first*	**souvent** *often*
d'habitude *usually*	**tard** *late*
demain matin *tomorrow morning*	**tôt** *early*
demain soir *tomorrow evening*	**tout de suite** *right away*
encore *still, yet, again*	

➤➤➤➤➤

Adverbs of time usually follow the verb directly, but some of them, such as **après, encore une fois, enfin, maintenant, quelquefois, souvent,** can be placed at the beginning of a sentence.

Mon chat dort **souvent** sur mon lit. } *My cat **often** sleeps on my bed.*
Souvent, mon chat dort sur mon lit.

■ Many phrases referring to points in time function as adverbial phrases.

1. The days of the week and the days of the week with the definite article:

—Tu ne travailles pas **lundi?**   *You're not working **this Monday**?*
—Non, je ne travaille jamais **le lundi.**   *No, I never work **on Mondays.***

2. Parts of the day and week with the definite article or a demonstrative adjective:

le matin *in the morning*

l'après-midi *in the afternoon*

le soir *in the evening*

la nuit *at night*

le lendemain *the day after, the next day*

la veille *the evening before, the day before*

ce week-end *this weekend*

cette année *this year*

3. Phrases with **prochain** and **dernier:**

la semaine/l'année prochaine *next week/year*

la semaine/l'année dernière *last week/year*

mercredi prochain *next Wednesday*

mercredi dernier *last Wednesday*

4. Phrases with **tout** and **chaque:**

toute la journée *all day long*

tous les jours *every day*

toutes les semaines *every week*

chaque jour/chaque semaine *each day/each week*

5. Phrases with **fois:**

une fois *once*

deux fois *twice*

trois fois *three times*

une fois par semaine *once a week*

B. L'intrus. Cross out the adverb or adverbial phrase that does not belong in each group.

1. après-demain   demain   le lendemain   hier

2. quelquefois   jamais   souvent   d'habitude

3. l'année dernière   bientôt   tout de suite   maintenant

4. rarement   une fois par an   toujours   jamais

5. la veille   mardi prochain   avant-hier   autrefois

C. Quand ça? Correct these mistaken impressions with a French adverb or adverbial phrase that is the equivalent of the English words in parentheses. Replace words in italics by object pronouns in your answers.

Modèle   —Monique achète *des cadeaux* aujourd'hui, n'est-ce pas? *(tomorrow)*
     ➤ —Non, elle en achète demain.

1. —Elle va souvent *au cinéma*, n'est-ce pas? *(seldom)*

    — _____

2. —Tu fais *du jogging* tous les jours, n'est-ce pas? *(three times a week)*

    — _____

3. —Tu fais *tes devoirs* le soir, n'est-ce pas? *(in the afternoon)*

    — _____

4. —Jacques va *à Paris* demain, n'est-ce pas? *(day after tomorrow)*

    — _____

5. —Sylvie fait *les courses* cet après-midi, n'est-ce pas? *(tomorrow morning)*

    — _____

6. —Tu fais *le ménage* tous les jours, n'est-ce pas? *(once a week)*

    — _____

7. —Richard et Lucille saluent toujours *le professeur*, n'est-ce pas? *(never)*

    — _____

8. —Il travaille *au bureau* le matin seulement, n'est-ce pas? *(all day)*

    — _____

D. Qu'est-ce que vous faites et quand le faites-vous? Selecting elements from each of the three columns below, write eight sentences about what you, your friends, and your family do. Make sure each of your sentences has an element from each column. You may substitute other elements if you choose.

column 1	column 2	column 3
moi, je	arriver à l'école	_____ fois par semaine
mes amis et moi, nous	faire ses devoirs	tous les jours
mon ami _____	passer l'été à la campagne	tous les ans
mon amie _____	faire du jogging	le matin/le soir
les étudiants	faire de l'exercice	l'après-midi
le professeur	faire du sport	tous les soirs/les matins
le directeur	faire de la barque	le samedi/le dimanche
	aller au cinéma	quelquefois
	aller voir des matchs	souvent
	étudier	demain/après-demain
		la semaine prochaine
		lundi, mardi, etc. prochain
		le mois prochain

1. _____

2. _____

3. _____

4. _____

5. _____

6. _____

7. _____

8. _____

III. Adverbs of Place

■ Here is a list of some common adverbs and adverbial phrases of place. Note that some of them, such as **derrière** and **devant** can also function as prepositions when followed directly by a noun: **derrière le lycée, devant le cinéma.** These prepositional phrases usually function as adverbs.

dedans *inside*

dehors *outside*

derrière *behind, in back*

devant *in front*

en bas *downstairs*

en haut *upstairs*

là-bas *there, over there*

partout *everywhere*

E. Antonymes. Write the words that mean the opposite of the adverbs of place below.

1. près   _____

2. en haut   _____

3. dedans   _____

4. ici   _____

5. derrière   _____

F. Expansion. Expand each of the following sentences by adding the French equivalent of the adverb of place in parentheses.

Modèle   Bernard travaille. *(outside)* ➤ Bernard travaille dehors.

1. Nous allons manger. *(inside)*

   _____

2. Nous avons besoin de ce livre. Nous le cherchons. *(everywhere)*

   _____

3. Voilà le stade. *(over there)*

   _____

4. Le chien joue. *(in back)*

   _____

5. Le bébé dort. *(upstairs)*

   _____

6. Marc et ses amis écoutent des cassettes. *(downstairs)*

   _____

IV. Adverbs ending in *-ment*

■ The suffix **-ment** can be used to form adverbs from adjectives in French, much as the suffix *-ly* does in English (e.g., wonderful ➤ wonderfully). The suffix **-ment** is added to the feminine form of the adjective.

masculine	feminine ➤ adverb	
lent	lente ➤	lentement *slowly*
heureux	heureuse ➤	heureusement *happily, fortunately*
doux	douce ➤	doucement *softly, gently*

If the masculine form of the adjective already ends in a vowel, the suffix **-ment** is added to the masculine.

masculine	adverb
absolu ➤	absolument *absolutely*
facile ➤	facilement *easily*
vrai ➤	vraiment *really, truly*

Some adverbs are formed irregularly.

bon ➤	bien *well*
constant ➤	constamment *constantly*
courant ➤	couramment *fluently*
énorme ➤	énormément *enormously: an awful lot, very much*
gentil ➤	gentiment *in a friendly way, nicely*
mauvais ➤	mal *badly*
récent ➤	récemment *recently*

Notes

1. **Vraiment** often modifies adjectives and other adverbs.

Elle est **vraiment** intelligente.	*She's **really** intelligent.*
Il parle **vraiment** bien.	*He speaks **really** well.*

2. Since the adverb **très** cannot be combined with **beaucoup**, **énormément** is used instead to mean *very much*.

Nous avons **énormément** de travail.	*We have an **awful lot** of work.*
Elle m'aide **énormément**.	*She helps me **very much**.*

G. Aux adverbes! Write the adverb corresponding to each of these adjectives and give the English translation of each adverb that you write.

	Adjective	Adverb	English translation of adverb
1.	généreux	_____	_____
2.	cruel	_____	_____

3. impoli   _____   _____

4. raisonnable   _____   _____

5. timide   _____   _____

6. actuel   _____   _____

7. bête   _____   _____

8. malheureux   _____   _____

9. merveilleux   _____   _____

10. gentil   _____   _____

H. Les adverbes à l'œuvre. Rewrite the following sentences, adding the necessary adverbs so that they express the ideas in parentheses.

1. Il me salue. *(in a friendly way)*

_____

2. Dans cette rue il y a des voitures. *(an awful lot of cars)*

_____

3. Pour réussir il faut travailler. *(seriously)*

_____

4. C'est un garçon intelligent. *(really intelligent)*

_____

5. Elle lit le français. *(fluently)*

_____

6. Ils nous téléphonent. *(constantly)*

_____

7. Ce touriste parle. *(badly)*

_____

8. Il faut répondre au professeur. *(politely)*

_____

L'industrie automobile

The French auto industry is the world's fourth largest after Japan, the United States, and Germany. France's two car companies, **PSA Peugeot** and **Renault,** produce over 3,000,000 vehicles a year, about 2,800,000 of them private cars and over 300,000 trucks. Sixty percent of the cars and trucks produced in France are exported, and the auto industry provides 300,000 jobs for French workers. Although French cars are popular abroad, 40% of the cars bought by French people are imported from other countries, mainly Germany and Italy.

V. Adverbs with the *passé composé*

- In the **passé composé,** adverbs of manner such as **bien, mal,** etc. and adverbs of quantity such as **beaucoup, assez, trop,** etc. come between the auxiliary verb and the past participle.

  —Tu as **beaucoup** étudié?   *Did you study **a lot**?*
  —Oui, mais j'ai **mal** dormi.   *Yes, but I slept **badly**.*

- Other short adverbs such as **déjà, encore, rarement, souvent, toujours, vite** also come between the auxiliary verb and past participle.

  —Vous avez **déjà** cherché vos clés?   *Have you **already** looked for your keys?*

  —Oui, mais je ne les ai **pas encore** trouvées.   *Yes, but I haven't found them **yet**.*

- Adverbs of time such as **demain, aujourd'hui,** and **hier** either follow the past participle or come at the beginning of the sentence for emphasis.

  J'ai travaillé **aujourd'hui. Demain** je sors.   *I worked **today. Tomorrow** I'm going out.*

- Adverbs ending in **-ment,** especially the short ones, are usually placed between the auxiliary verb and the past participle.

  —Tu as **suffisamment** étudié le poème?   *Did you study that poem **enough**?*
  —Oui, et je l'ai **vraiment** compris.   *Yes, and I **really** understood it.*

I. **Les amis partent en vacances.** Rewrite this story about Jacques and his friends leaving on vacation together in the **passé composé.** Pay special attention to the position of the adverbs and adverbial phrases.

1. Jacques se lève de bonne heure.

    _____

2. Il téléphone tout de suite à ses amis.

3. Ils décident de partir ce matin.

_____

4. Ils se retrouvent vite.

_____

5. Ils se mettent déjà en route.

_____

6. Ils ne sortent pas encore de la ville.

_____

7. Ces amis passent souvent les vacances ensemble.

_____

8. Ils s'amusent toujours.

_____

J. **Questions personnelles.** Answer the following questions using one of the adverbs suggested.

1. Est-ce que vous étudiez sérieusement? Attentivement?

_____

2. Est-ce que vos amis vous téléphonent constamment ou rarement?

_____

3. Est-ce que vous faites de l'exercice tous les jours ou une ou deux fois par semaine?

_____

4. Est-ce que vous courez vite ou lentement?

_____

5. Combien est-ce que vous avez travaillé aujourd'hui? Beaucoup, assez, trop, ou peu?

_____

K. **Composition.** In a paragraph of eight to ten sentences, describe a get-together that you and your friends had. Use as many adverbs and adverbial phrases as possible to tell *how, where,* and *when* the gathering took place. Use adverbs of manner to describe *how* people spoke, acted, and reacted.

Review of Prepositions; Geographical Names

I. Prepositions

■ The most common French prepositions are

à *at, to*	**devant** *in front of*
après *after*	**en** *in, made of*
avant *before*	**entre** *between*
avec *with*	**jusqu'à** *until*
chez *at the house of*	**pour** *for, in order to*
dans *in*	**sans** *without*
de *from, of*	**sous** *under*
derrière *in back of, behind*	**sur** *on*

■ Remember that the prepositions **à** and **de** contract with the definite articles **le** and **les.**

à + le ➤ **au**	de + le ➤ **du**
à + les ➤ **aux**	de + les ➤ **des**

There are no contractions with the articles **la, l'.**

Notes

1. **À** marks distance in time and space.

J'habite **à** 20 kilomètres de Lyon.	*I live 20 kilometers from Lyon.*
Mon lycée est **à** dix minutes de chez moi.	*My school is ten minutes from my house.*

2. **À** labels the principal ingredient or the characteristic feature.

un tarte **aux** pommes	*an apple pastry*
le jeune homme **aux** cheveux blonds	*the young man with blond hair*

3. **Changer de** + singular noun means *to change (from one thing to another).*

changer **de** train/d'avion	*to change trains/planes*
changer **de** vêtements	*to change one's clothes*
changer **d'**avis	*to change one's mind*

4. **En** labels the material of which something is made.

une jupe **en** laine	*a wool skirt*
une montre **en** or	*a gold watch*

5. **Sur** often means *about*.

se renseigner **sur** les tarifs	*to get information **about** fares*
un livre **sur** Paris	*a book **about** Paris*

6. The infinitive is the form of the verb that follows a preposition.

Je ne vais pas réussir **sans étudier.**	*I won't pass **without studying.***

7. **Pour** before an infinitive means *in order to*.

Je te téléphone **pour** te demander un service.	*I'm calling to ask you for a favor.*

8. No preposition is used after verbs of motion before an infinitive.

Maman **descend faire** les courses.	*Mother **is going downstairs to do** the errands.*

A. Complétez! Complete these sentences with the missing prepositions.

1. Quand on ira à Marseille, on descendra _____ nos cousins.

   a. devant   b. sous   c. chez

2. Je m'ennuie dans ce bureau. Je veux changer _____ travail.

   a. de   b. pour   c. jusqu'à

3. Odile est _____ Paris. Elle y est née.

   a. en   b. de   c. après

4. Quand il fait chaud, je mets des chemisiers _____ coton.

   a. à   b. avec   c. en

5. Comme dessert, je voudrais une glace _____ chocolat.

   a. en   b. de   c. au

6. J'ai besoin d'un article _____ les nouveaux ordinateurs.

   a. de   b. sur   c. sous

7. Nous avons loué une voiture _____ aller à Paris.

   a. pour   b. no preposition necessary   c. avec

8. Il y a un café _____ 300 mètres d'ici.

   a. jusqu'à   b. dans   c. à

II. Compound Prepositions

■ French also has phrases ending in **de** that serve as prepositions.

à cause de *because of*	**au sujet de** *about*
à côté de *next to*	**en face de** *opposite, across from*
au bout de *at the end of*	**près de** *near*
au coin de *at the corner of*	**loin de** *far from*
au milieu de *in the middle of*	

■ The contractions **du** and **des** are used when the articles **le** and **les** follow these prepositions: **loin du village, au sujet des cours.**

B. Complétez! Complete these sentences with the missing prepositions.

1. Tu ne peux pas aller à la gare à pied. C'est _____ ici.

   a. jusqu'à   b. près d'   c. loin d'

2. Allez _____ la rue et tournez à gauche.

   a. au bout de   b. au milieu de   c. en face de

3. Tout le monde est malade _____ froid qu'il fait.

   a. à côté du   b. à cause du   c. au sujet du

4. Il y a un supermarché _____ notre immeuble. On traverse la rue pour acheter à manger.

   a. en face de   b. à cause dc   c. au milieu du

5. Ils n'ont rien dit _____ problème.

   a. près du   b. au sujet du   c. au bout du

III. Prepositions before Infinitives

Some verbs require either the preposition **à** or **de** before a following infinitive. Here are the most important ones. (**qqn = quelqu'un, qqch = quelque chose**)

■ Verb + **à** + infinitive

aider qqn à *to help someone to*	**se mettre à** *to begin to*
apprendre à *to learn how to*	**passer son temps à** *to spend one's*
s'attendre à *to expect to*	*time doing*
commencer à *to begin to*	**se préparer à** *to get ready to*
continuer à *to continue doing something*	**réussir à** *to succeed in*
se décider à *to make up one's mind to*	**tenir à** *to insist on*
inviter qqn à *to invite (someone) to*	

- Verb + **de** + infinitive

accepter de *to agree to*	**mériter de** *to deserve to*
avoir l'intention de *to intend to*	**oublier de** *to forget to*
avoir peur de *to be afraid to*	**promettre de** *to promise to*
choisir de *to choose to*	**refuser de** *to refuse to*
décider de *to decide to*	**regretter de** *to regret*
essayer de *to try to*	

- Note also the expression **venir de faire quelque chose** *(to have just done something)*.

C. **Étudier ou sortir?** Find out why Marie may not be prepared for tomorrow's test by completing the following sentences with the missing prepositions.

1. Marie a l'intention _____ travailler ce soir.

2. Elle a décidé _____ rester chez elle.

3. Elle va passer son temps _____ étudier.

4. Marie commence _____ travailler.

5. Jacques téléphone et invite Marie _____ sortir.

6. D'abord Marie refuse _____ abandonner son travail.

7. Elle essaie _____ penser à son examen.

8. Mais Jacques réussit _____ la convaincre.

9. Marie accepte _____ sortir.

10. Elle continue _____ travailler jusqu'à l'arrivée de Jacques.

D. Tout récent. The Rocard family is getting ready to go to sleep. Mrs. Rocard is checking to see that all the chores are done. Say that the things she asks about have just happened using the expression **venir de.**

Modèle —Luc est déjà parti?
➢ —Oui, il vient de partir.

À la maison

éteindre (past participle **éteint**) *to put out*

l'évier (masc.) *sink*

faire la vaisselle *to do the dishes*

fermer à clé *to lock*

la lumière *light*

rentrer *to bring in* (conjugated with **avoir** with this meaning)

---

1. Les enfants se sont déjà couchés?

   _____

2. Rosalie a déjà fait la vaisselle?

   _____

3. Tu as déjà mis la voiture dans le garage?

   _____

4. Vous avez fermé les fenêtres?

   _____

5. On a rentré le chat?

   _____

6. On a nettoyé l'évier?

   _____

7. Tu as fermé la porte à clé?

   _____

8. On a éteint les lumières du salon?

   _____

IV. Prepositions with Names of Places

Before names of cities, states, provinces, and countries, French uses the same preposition to express *to* and *in* (direction and location), either à (au, aux) or **en.**

- French uses à before the names of cities.

  aller à Paris, à Marseille, à New York   *to go **to** Paris, **to** Marseilles, **to** New York*

  être à Paris, à Marseille, à New York   *to be **in** Paris, **in** Marseilles, **in** New York*

- French uses **en** before the names of countries, states, and provinces that are feminine.

  aller **en** France, **en** Normandie, **en** Virginie   *to go **to** France, **to** Normandy, **to** Virginia*

  travailler **en** France, **en** Normandie, **en** Virginie   *to work **in** France, **in** Normandy, **in** Virginia*

- French uses **à** + definite article to express *to/in* before the names of countries, states, and provinces that are masculine or plural.

  aller **aux** États-Unis, **au** Mexique, **au** Portugal   *to go **to** the United States, **to** Mexico, **to** Portugal*

  être **aux** États-Unis, **au** Mexique, **au** Portugal   *to be **in** the United States, **in** Mexico, **in** Portugal*

- The preposition **en** is used before masculine singular countries beginning with a vowel.

  en Haïti, **en** Israël, **en** Iran   *to/in Haiti, Israel, Iran*

  To express *from,* French uses **de** (**du, de la, des, de l'**).

- **De** is used before the names of cities, before feminine countries, and before masculine countries beginning with a vowel.

  de Paris, **de** France, **d'**Israël   *from Paris, from France, from Israel*

- **De** + the definite article is used to express *from* before the names of countries, states, and provinces that are masculine or plural.

  des États-Unis, **du** Mexique, **du** Portugal   *from the United States, from Mexico, from Portugal*

E. On voyage! Tell where each of these students is from and where he or she is now.

Modèle   Marc/Paris/New York

    ➤ Marc est de Paris. Il est maintenant à New York.

1. Christine/Philadelphie/Londres

_____

2. Sergio/Italie/France

_____

➤➤➤➤➤

3. Maria/Mexique/Espagne

_____

4. Philippe/Montréal/Rome

_____

5. Kimberley/États-Unis/Japon

_____

6. Luc/Suisse/Chine

_____

7. Irina/Russie/Amérique

_____

8. Shimon/Israël/Angleterre

_____

V. More on Prepositions with Place Names

■ Cities that have an article as part of their name keep the article after **à** and **de.**

Le Havre ➢ **au** Havre, **du** Havre

La Nouvelle-Orléans ➢ à **La** Nouvelle-Orléans, **de La** Nouvelle-Orléans

■ Other cities with a definite article in their name: **Le** Caire *(Cairo)*, **La** Rochelle, **La** Havane *(Havana)*.

■ Most islands take **à** and **de**; some islands have a definite article in their names.

à **la** Guadeloupe/**de la** Guadeloupe	*to, in Guadeloupe/from Guadeloupe*
à **la** Martinique/**de la** Martinique	*to, in Martinique/from Martinique*
à Porto Rico/**de** Porto Rico	*to, in Puerto Rico/from Puerto Rico*
BUT: **en/de** Corse	*to, in/from Corsica*

■ When a place name is modified, it must take the definite article. The prepositions **à** and **en** are replaced by **dans.**

dans la France du XIXᵉ siècle	*in nineteenth-century France*
dans le Canada colonial	*in colonial Canada*

- The prepositions **en** and **de** are used before those American states that are grammatically feminine.

    en/de Californie, **en/de** Caroline du Nord/du Sud, **en/de** Géorgie, **en/de** Floride, **en/de** Louisiane, **en/de** Pennsylvanie, **en/de** Virginie, **en/de** Virginie Occidentale *(West Virginia)*

- Other American states are masculine and take **dans le** or **au** if they begin with a consonant, **dans l'** or **en** if they begin with a vowel:

    dans le Texas/**au** Texas, **du** Texas

    dans l'Alabama/**en** Alabama, **de l'**Alabama/**d'**Alabama

- Note the following geographical names that might cause confusion.

le New York	*New York State*
New York	*New York City*
le Québec	*Quebec Province*
Québec	*Quebec City*
le Mexique	*Mexico (country)*
Mexico	*Mexico City*

F. Un été à l'étranger. These French teenagers have found summer jobs abroad. Tell what French city they are from and where they are working.

Modèle   Julie/Paris; Angleterre/Londres
  ➤ Julie est de Paris. Elle travaille en Angleterre, à Londres.

1. Solange/Marseille; États-Unis/Washington

    _____

2. Richard/Strasbourg; Italie/Milan

    _____

3. Arnaud/Lille; Japon/Tokyo

    _____

4. Caroline/La Rochelle; Brésil/Rio de Janeiro

    _____

5. Suzanne/Lyon; Égypte/Le Caire

    _____

6. Maurice/Le Havre; Le Québec/Québec

    _____

➤➤➤➤➤

7. Janine/Clermont-Ferrand; Californie/San Francisco

_____

8. Gérard/Biarritz; Canada/Montréal

_____

9. Sophie/Grenoble; Mexique/Mexico

_____

10. Daniel/Rouen; Louisiane/La Nouvelle-Orléans

_____

G. Questions personnelles

1. Est-ce qu'il y a des étudiants étrangers dans votre école? D'où sont-ils?

_____

2. Est-ce que vous avez de la famille qui habite loin de chez vous? Qui et où exactement?

_____

3. Vous habitez à quelle distance de l'école?

_____

4. Dans votre chambre, où gardez-vous vos livres?

_____

5. Où est-ce qu'on mange chez vous?

_____

H. Composition.

Describe either your room or the classroom. Locate objects and people relative to other things so as to use as many prepositions as possible. Write eight to ten sentences.

The Future and the Conditional

I. Future Tense

■ You already know how to express future actions using **aller** + infinitive.

Ils **vont partir** ce week-end.   *They **are going to leave** this weekend.*

A more formal way to express future plans is with the future tense.

Elles **partiront** après le dîner.   *They **will leave** after dinner.*

■ The future tense in French is formed by adding the following endings to the infinitive: **-ai, -as, -a, -ons, -ez, -ont.**

FUTURE OF **PARLER**

je parler**ai**	nous parler**ons**
tu parler**as**	vous parler**ez**
il/elle/on parler**a**	ils/elles parler**ont**

If the infinitive of the verb ends in **-e,** that **-e** is dropped before the future endings are added.

FUTURE OF **RENDRE**

je rendr**ai**	nous rendr**ons**
tu rendr**as**	vous rendr**ez**
il/elle/on rendr**a**	ils/elles rendr**ont**

■ Some verbs have an irregular stem in the future tense. These verbs have regular endings, however.

aller *(to go)* ➤ j'**irai**

avoir *(to have)* ➤ j'**aurai**

courir *(to run)* ➤ je **courrai**

devoir *(to owe; to be obliged to)* ➤ je **devrai**

envoyer *(to send)* ➤ j'**enverrai**

être *(to be)* ➤ je **serai**

faire *(to make; to do)* ➤ je **ferai**

pouvoir *(to be able to)* ➤ je **pourrai**

recevoir *(to receive)* ➤ je **recevrai**

savoir *(to know)* ➤ je **saurai**

tenir *(to hold)* ➤ je **tiendrai**

venir *(to come)* ➤ je **viendrai**

voir *(to see)* ➤ je **verrai**

vouloir *(to want)* ➤ je **voudrai**

Note also the following future forms:

il faut *(it is necessary to)* ➤ il **faudra**

il y a *(there is/are)* ➤ il y **aura**

il pleut *(it is raining)* ➤ il **pleuvra**

- ■ -**Er** verbs that change **e** to **è** before a mute **e** in the present (such as **acheter**) or that double their final consonant before a mute **e** (such as **appeler**) have the same change in all persons of the future tense.

  acheter ➢ j'**achèterai**

  appeler ➢ j'**appellerai**

  jeter ➢ je **jetterai**

- ■ Verbs such as **espérer** *(to hope)* and **préférer** retain **é** in all persons of the future tense.

  espérer ➢ j'**espérerai**

  préférer ➢ je **préférerai**

A. C'est pour demain. Your friend asks if these things have already happened. You tell your friend no, they will happen tomorrow. Replace any object nouns by the appropriate object pronouns.

Modèle　—Jean est déjà arrivé?
　　　　　➢ —Non, il arrivera demain.

1. —Tu as déjà pris les billets?

   —_____

2. —Chantal et toi, vous avez déjà fait le ménage?

   —_____

3. —Christine a déjà vu le film?

   —_____

4. —Les enfants ont déjà appelé leurs amis?

   —_____

5. —Tu as déjà acheté des vêtements pour l'été?

   —_____

6. —J'ai déjà reçu le paquet? *(Tu...)*

   —_____

7. —Marianne est déjà revenue?

   —_____

8. —Toi et Marc, vous êtes déjà allés danser?

   —_____

B. Projets pour l'été. Use the future tense to tell what these people will do this summer.

Modèle Olivier/rester chez lui ➤ Olivier restera chez lui.

1. mes parents et moi/faire un voyage au Canada

   _____

2. mon amie Sandrine/aller en Europe

   _____

3. Albert/avoir un emploi chez son oncle

   _____

4. Corinne et Justine/suivre des cours

   _____

5. toi/voir tes amis

   _____

6. vos cousins/venir chez vous

   _____

7. ma sœur et moi/faire du sport

   _____

8. moi/devoir étudier pour mon baccalauréat

   _____

C. Vous n'êtes pas sûr(e). Your friend wants to know if certain things are going to happen or not. Tell your friend in each case that you don't know using **je ne sais pas si** + future.

Modèle —Marie va partir ou non?
        ➤ —Je ne sais pas si elle partira.

1. —Tu vas aller ou non?

   — _____

2. —Elles vont rentrer ou non?

   — _____

➤➤➤➤➤

3. —Ta mère va descendre ou non?

   —_____

4. —Louise et toi, vous allez sortir ou non?

   —_____

5. —Je vais réussir ou non?

   —_____

6. —Nicolas et moi, nous allons devoir rester ou non?

   —_____

7. —Le petit Julien va préférer rester avec nous ou non?

   —_____

8. —Toi, tu vas acheter le journal ou non?

   —_____

II. The Conditional

■ The conditional in French expresses the idea *would do something*.

Vous **seriez** un excellent cuisinier.   *You **would be** an excellent chef.*

■ The conditional is formed by adding the endings of the imperfect
(**-ais, -ais, -ait, -ions, -iez, -aient**) to the infinitive. As with the future,
infinitives ending in **-e** drop that **-e** before adding the endings of the
conditional.

CONDITIONAL OF PARLER

je parler**ais**	nous parler**ions**
tu parler**ais**	vous parler**iez**
il/elle/on parler**ait**	ils/elles parler**aient**

CONDITIONAL OF RENDRE

je rendr**ais**	nous rendr**ions**
tu rendr**ais**	vous rendr**iez**
il/elle/on rendr**ait**	ils/elles rendr**aient**

■ Any irregularity in the future stem also appears in the conditional.

acheter ➤ j'**achèterais**	espérer ➤ j'**espérerais**	savoir ➤ je **saurais**
aller ➤ **j'irais**	être ➤ je **serais**	tenir ➤ je **tiendrais**
appeler ➤ j'**appellerais**	faire ➤ je **ferais**	venir ➤ je **viendrais**
avoir ➤ **j'aurais**	jeter ➤ je **jetterais**	voir ➤ je **verrais**
courir ➤ je **courrais**	pouvoir ➤ je **pourrais**	vouloir ➤ je **voudrais**
devoir ➤ je **devrais**	préférer ➤ je **préférerais**	
envoyer ➤ j'**enverrais**	recevoir ➤ je **recevrais**	

AND:

il faut ➤ il **faudrait**   il y a ➤ il y **aurait**   il pleut ➤ il **pleuvrait**

D. Pas moi. Say that each of these people would not do the thing mentioned. Use the conditional and replace object nouns in italics by the corresponding pronoun.

Modèle   Jacqueline lit *la revue. (Claire)*
➤ Claire ne la lirait pas.

1. Suzanne écrit *à Florence. (moi)*

   _____

2. Nos amis étudient *à la bibliothèque. (nous)*

   _____

3. Luc boit *du citron pressé. (toi)*

   _____

4. Moi, je réponds *aux questions de François. (ses copains)*

   _____

5. Solange jette *ses rédactions. (vous)*

   _____

6. Vous achetez *des journaux. (Christelle)*

   _____

E. Des vacances idéales. Pierre is imagining an ideal camping trip with his family and friends. He tells what each one would do using the conditional.

Modèle   nous/partir de bonne heure
➤ Nous partirions de bonne heure.

Le camping

la boîte de conserve *can*	**le feu** *fire*
dresser une tente *to set up a tent*	**garer la voiture** *to park the car*

---

1. nous/arriver avant midi

   _____

2. mes parents/garer la voiture

   _____

3. moi/dresser la tente

   _____

4. toi/faire un feu

   _____

5. Charles/ouvrir les boîtes de conserves

   _____

6. toi et Paul/préparer le dîner

   _____

7. nous/manger tous ensemble

   _____

8. Jacques/jouer de la guitare

   _____

9. tout le monde/chanter

   _____

10. nous/se coucher à neuf heures

    _____

III. Conditional Sentences

- A conditional sentence consists of two parts: a **si** *(if)*-clause and a result clause. To express that something probably will happen, you use the present tense in the **si**-clause and the present, imperative, or future in the result clause.

Ne **sors** pas s'il **fait** mauvais.

*Don't **go out** if the weather **is** bad.*

S'il **arrive** avant sept heures, tu le **verras.**

*If he **arrives** before seven, you'll **see** him.*

- To express what things would be like if circumstances were different, in other words, something that is contrary to fact, French uses the imperfect tense in the **si**-clause and the conditional in the result clause.

Il **viendrait** s'il **pouvait.**

*He'd **come** if he **could.** (But he can't.)*

Si on n'**avait** pas tant de devoirs, nous **sortirions.**

*If we **didn't have** so much homework, we **would go out.** (But we do have so much homework.)*

- The following chart summarizes these possibilities.

Conditional sentences: summary of tenses	
Si-clause	Result clause
present	present, future, or imperative
imperfect	conditional

F. **Mangeons.** For each pair of clauses, write a sentence (a.) that tells what may well happen (**si**-clause in the present, result clause in the future) and a second one (b.) that tells what is unlikely to happen (**si**-clause in the imperfect, result clause in the conditional).

Modèle *Si*-clause   **Result clause**
Tu veux des bonbons.   J'en achète.

a. Si tu veux des bonbons, j'en achèterai.
b. Si tu voulais des bonbons, j'en achèterais.

Si-clause   **Result clause**

1. Maman a besoin de lait.   Elle descend.

a. _____

b. _____

2. Nous voulons manger.   Maman met la table.

a. _____

b. _____

➤➤➤➤➤

3. Tu as faim. Je te sers du fromage.

a. _____

b. _____

4. Jacques veut manger quelque chose. Il peut regarder dans le frigo.

a. _____

b. _____

5. Les enfants ont soif. Nous leur donnons du jus.

a. _____

b. _____

G. **Il faut se soigner!** Mme Guillaume is giving her family some advice about health. Write what she says as conditional sentences that are contrary to the facts as given.

Modèle Tu écoutes tant de rock. Tu as mal à la tête.
➤ Si tu n'écoutais pas tant de rock, tu n'aurais pas mal à la tête.

La santé	
attraper *to catch*	**le médicament** *medication*
le courant d'air *draft*	**mincir** *to get slim*
être en forme *to be in shape*	**pieds nus** *barefoot*
être grippé *to have the flu*	**le rhume** *head cold*
guérir *to cure; get well*	**sous la pluie** *in the rain*

1. Vous ne prenez pas vos vitamines. Vous êtes toujours fatigués.

_____

2. Tu ne fermes pas les fenêtres. Il y a des courants d'air.

_____

3. Tu marches pieds nus. Tu te fais mal au pied.

_____

4. Ton frère ne fait pas d'exercice. Il n'est pas en forme.

_____

5. Nous ne mangeons pas de légumes. Nous ne mincissons pas.

   _____

6. Les enfants sortent sous la pluie. Ils attrapent des rhumes.

   _____

7. Grand-père ne prend pas ses médicaments. Il ne guérit pas.

   _____

8. Je ne vais pas chez le médecin. Je ne sais pas si je suis grippée.

   _____

H. Problèmes d'argent. Use a conditional sentence containing a **si**-clause in the imperfect and a result clause in the conditional to tell how each of these money problems could be solved.

Modèle   Tu n'as pas ta carte bleue. Tu ne peux pas acheter cette robe.
   ➤ Si tu avais ta carte bleue, tu pourrais acheter cette robe.

Le monde de l'argent

la carte bancaire *bank card*	**emprunter** *to borrow*
la carte bleue *French credit card*	**endetté** *in debt*
le compte en banque *bank account*	**rembourser** *to pay back*
déposer *to deposit*	**toucher** *to cash*

---

1. Jeanne ne nous prête pas d'argent. Nous ne pouvons pas sortir.

   _____

2. La banque n'est pas ouverte. Je ne peux pas déposer mon argent.

   _____

3. Je n'ai pas ma carte bancaire. On ne touche pas mon chèque.

   _____

4. Mon minitel ne fonctionne pas. Je n'ai pas d'accès à mon compte en banque.

   _____

➤➤➤➤➤

5. Je ne réussis pas à trouver mon porte-feuille. Je ne te rembourse pas.

_____

6. Il emprunte tant d'argent. Il est toujours endetté.

_____

L'argent, le crédit et la banque

- **Carte bleue** (affiliated with Visa) and **Eurocard** (affiliated with Master-card) are the two most popular credit cards in France. American Express and Diner's Club are also used.
- The **Minitel** is a home computer station connected to the telephone lines like a modem that gives users access to a range of services, including on-line banking. There are about 7 million Minitels in use in France.

I. **Questions personnelles.** Answer the following questions in complete French sentences.

Qu'est-ce que vous feriez...

1. ... si vous aviez beaucoup d'argent?

_____

_____

2. ... s'il ne vous fallait pas assister à l'école?

_____

_____

3. ... si vous aviez trois examens la semaine prochaine?

_____

_____

J. **Composition.** Write about your future plans. Use the future to tell what you will do and conditional sentences to tell what you would do depending on circumstances.

The Present Subjunctive

I. Forms of the Present Subjunctive

■ The present subjunctive is used in French in dependent clauses after certain verbs and expressions. The endings of the present subjunctive are the same for almost all French verbs: -e, -es, -e, -ions, -iez, -ent. These endings are added to the subjunctive stem, which is the **nous** form of the present tense minus the -ons ending. For example, **finir**: nous **finissons̸** ➤ que je **finisse.**

■ The present subjunctive is used after **il faut que** *(it is necessary).*

Il faut **que tu finisses** le devoir avant de partir.	*It is necessary **for you to finish** the work before leaving.*

■ Here are the subjunctive forms of regular verbs ending in **-er, -ir,** and **-re.**

RENTRER	FINIR	DESCENDRE
que je **rentre**	que je **finisse**	que je **descende**
que tu **rentres**	que tu **finisses**	que tu **descendes**
qu'il/elle/on **rentre**	qu'il/elle/on **finisse**	qu'il/elle/on **descende**
que nous **rentrions**	que nous **finissions**	que nous **descendions**
que vous **rentriez**	que vous **finissiez**	que vous **descendiez**
qu'ils/elles **rentrent**	qu'ils/elles **finissent**	qu'ils/elles **descendent**

■ **-Er** verbs that have changes in the vowel in the present tense such as **acheter** and **jeter** have the same changes in the present subjunctive: **que j'achète, que je jette** *vs.* **que vous achetiez, que vous jetiez.** Note that in **-er** verbs, the present subjunctive and the present indicative are identical except for the **nous** and **vous** forms. For other verbs, the present subjunctive is different from the present indicative except for the **ils/elles** form, which is the same in both.

■ Most irregular verbs follow the same pattern as regular verbs in the present subjunctive. They add the subjunctive endings to the **nous** form of the present tense minus the **-ons** ending.

DIRE	ÉCRIRE	SORTIR
que je **dise**	que j'**écrive**	que je **sorte**
que tu **dises**	que tu **écrives**	que tu **sortes**
qu'il/elle/on **dise**	qu'il/elle/on **écrive**	qu'il/elle/on **sorte**
que nous **disions**	que nous **écrivions**	que nous **sortions**
que vous **disiez**	que vous **écriviez**	que vous **sortiez**
qu'ils/elles **disent**	qu'ils/elles **écrivent**	qu'ils/elles **sortent**

- Irregular verbs such as **boire, venir,** and **prendre,** which have changes in the stem of the **nous** and **vous** forms of the present, have these changes in the present subjunctive as well.

BOIRE	VENIR	PRENDRE
que je **boive**	que je **vienne**	que je **prenne**
que tu **boives**	que tu **viennes**	que tu **prennes**
qu'il/elle/on **boive**	qu'il/elle/on **vienne**	qu'il/elle/on **prenne**
que nous **buvions**	que nous **venions**	que nous **prenions**
que vous **buviez**	que vous **veniez**	que vous **preniez**
qu'ils/elles **boivent**	qu'ils/elles **viennent**	qu'ils/elles **prennent**

- Compare similar changes in **recevoir, voir, croire.**

que je **reçoive** *vs.* que nous **recevions**

que je **voie** *vs.* que nous **voyions**

que je **croie** *vs.* que nous **croyions**

- The following verbs are irregular in the present subjunctive.

ÊTRE	AVOIR	SAVOIR
que je **sois**	que j'**aie**	que je **sache**
que tu **sois**	que tu **aies**	que tu **saches**
qu'il/elle/on **soit**	qu'il/elle/on **ait**	qu'il/elle/on **sache**
que nous **soyons**	que nous **ayons**	que nous **sachions**
que vous **soyez**	que vous **ayez**	que vous **sachiez**
qu'ils/elles **soient**	qu'ils/elles **aient**	qu'ils/elles **sachent**

POUVOIR	ALLER	FAIRE
que je **puisse**	que j'**aille**	que je **fasse**
que tu **puisses**	que tu **ailles**	que tu **fasses**
qu'il/elle/on **puisse**	qu'il/elle/on **aille**	qu'il/elle/on **fasse**
que nous **puissions**	que nous **allions**	que nous **fassions**
que vous **puissiez**	que vous **alliez**	que vous **fassiez**
qu'ils/elles **puissent**	qu'ils/elles **aillent**	qu'ils/elles **fassent**

A. Le va-et-vient. You've got a house full of people. Tell where each person should be, using **il faut que** + present subjunctive.

Modèle Jacques/monter ➤ Il faut que Jacques monte.

1. tu/descendre

   _____

2. nous/rentrer

   _____

3. Maurice/revenir

   _____

4. Alice et Monique/sortir

_____

5. vous/s'en aller

_____

6. nous/passer chez Lise

_____

7. je/être ici

_____

8. tu/partir

_____

B. Oui, il le faut. Mireille Lavallée asks her mother if she should do certain things. Her mother answers in each case that she must, using **il faut que.**

Modèle   —Je dois me coucher?
   ➤ —Oui, il faut que tu te couches.

1. —Je dois prendre ce médicament?

— _____

2. —Je dois boire ce jus?

— _____

3. —Je dois faire mes devoirs?

— _____

4. —Je dois finir mon dîner?

— _____

5. —Je dois attendre mon frère?

— _____

6. —Je dois écrire à ma tante?

— _____

➤➤➤➤➤

7. —Je dois lire ces chapitres?

    — _____

8. —Je dois savoir cette adresse?

    — _____

II. The Subjunctive to Express Desire, Will, or Necessity

■ The subjunctive is used in subordinate clauses after verbs such as **vouloir** and **préférer** that express the idea of wanting someone else to do something.

—Tu **veux que** je m'en aille?
—Non, je **préfère que** tu sois ici avec nous.

*Do you **want me to leave**?*
*No, I **prefer you to be** here with us.*

■ The following phrases express will or necessity and are followed by the subjunctive.

il est nécessaire que *it is necessary*

il est utile que *it is useful*

il est important que *it is important*

il faut que *it is necessary*

—**Il est nécessaire que** vous finissiez ce travail.
—**Il faut que** vous m'aidiez, alors.

***It's necessary for** you to finish this work.*
*Then you **have to help** me.*

■ The subjunctive is used after the following verbs of will or necessity.

aimer mieux que *to prefer*

préférer que *to prefer*

avoir besoin que *to need*

recommander que *to recommend*

empêcher que *to prevent*

souhaiter que *to wish*

exiger que *to demand*

suggérer que *to suggest*

ordonner que *to order*

vouloir que *to want*

permettre que *to allow*

—Tu **veux que** Louis parte?
—Non, je **préfère qu'**il nous attende.

*Do you **want** Louis to leave?*
*No, I **prefer** him to wait for us.*

■ If the subject of the dependent clause is the same as the subject of the main clause, then the infinitive, not the subjunctive, is used.

Je **veux qu'**il parte.
Je **veux** partir.

*I **want** him to leave.*
*I **want** to leave.*

■ The present subjunctive is used after all tenses of the verb in the main clause.

Elle **voulait** que tu reviennes.

*She **wanted** you to come back.*

Le médecin **a ordonné** que tu prennes ce médicament.

*The doctor **ordered** you to take this medicine.*

C. **Qu'est-ce que le professeur préfère?** Students ask their teacher if they may do certain things. She tells them using **préférer** + the present subjunctive that she prefers that they do something else. The teacher addresses individual students as **tu.**

Modèle   —Nous pouvons nous lever? *(rester assis)*
➤ —Je préfère que vous restiez assis.

1. —Je peux bavarder avec Chantal? *(lire)*

   —_____

2. —Pouvons-nous commencer nos devoirs? *(les faire chez vous)*

   —_____

3. —Je peux manger mon sandwich maintenant? *(attendre)*

   —_____

4. —Pouvons-nous faire une excursion vendredi? *(passer la journée ici)*

   —_____

5. —Je peux aller au terrain de sport? *(avoir un peu de patience)*

   —_____

6. —Pouvons-nous voir un film? *(étudier)*

   —_____

7. —Je peux lire mon roman? *(faire attention)*

   —_____

8. —Pouvons-nous sortir? *(finir votre travail)*

   —_____

D. **C'est exactement ce que je voulais.** Things are working out well for the big class reunion Louis planned. When people report what's going on, Louis says in each case that that's what he wanted to happen. Write out his reactions using **je voulais** + present subjunctive.

Modèle   —Odile et Janine vont rentrer aujourd'hui.
➤ —Parfait. Je voulais qu'elles rentrent.

1. —Marc va venir.

   —_____

2. —Solange va faire un gâteau.

   —_____

➤➤➤➤➤

3. —Moi, je vais être là en avance.

   — _____

4. —Charles et Philippe vont amener leurs cousins.

   — _____

5. —Anne Marie va mettre la table.

   — _____

6. —Nous, on va jouer de la guitare.

   — _____

7. —Claudette va appeler ses amies.

   — _____

8. —Nous, on va organiser des jeux.

   — _____

III. The Subjunctive after Expressions of Emotion and Personal Opinion

■ The subjunctive is used after phrases that express emotional reactions, such as

1. happiness and sadness

   je suis content(e)/heureux(se) que _I'm happy that_

   je suis triste/désolé(e) que _I'm sad/terribly sorry that_

   je regrette que _I'm sorry that_

2. fear and shame

   avoir peur que _to be afraid that_

   avoir honte que _to be ashamed that_

3. surprise

   il est surprenant que _it is surprising that_

   il est étonnant que _it is astonishing that_

   cela m'ennuie que _it annoys me that_

   il est ennuyeux/embêtant que _it's annoying that_

   —Je suis **content que** tout le monde puisse venir à la boum.   _I'm **happy that** everybody can come to the party._

   —Il est **surprenant que** personne ne soit pris.   _It's **surprising that** no one is busy._

■ The subjunctive is used after expressions such as the following that give one's opinion or evaluation.

peu importe que *it matters little that, it's unimportant that*

il vaut mieux que *it's better that*

il est logique/normal/naturel/juste que *it's logical/normal/natural/ right that*

c'est une chance que *it's lucky that*

ce n'est pas la peine que *it's not worth it that*

il est possible/impossible que *it's possible/impossible that*

il se peut que *it's possible that*

—Je suis **désolé** que tu ne puisses pas venir.	*I'm so **sorry** you can't come.*
—Moi aussi. Mais il **vaut mieux** que je fasse mes devoirs.	*Me too. But it's **better** for me to do my homework.*

E. Mme Gaubert n'est pas très contente. Mme Gaubert hoped everyone would be home for dinner, but there are complications. Write her reactions to what's happening.

Modèle   je suis fâchée/mon mari est en retard
➤ Je suis fâchée que mon mari soit en retard.

On dîne

la quiche *quiche, type of soufflé*   **le poulet rôti** *roast chicken*
s'abîmer *to spoil (of food)*

---

1. je suis contente/le dîner est prêt

   _____

2. il est surprenant/mes trois enfants ne sont pas là

   _____

3. il est ennuyeux/Jacques va à la bibliothèque

   _____

4. il se peut/Christine fait ses devoirs chez son amie Lise

   _____

5. il n'est pas logique/Michel a un match de football aujourd'hui

_____

6. il vaut mieux/je met tout dans le frigo

_____

7. j'ai peur/la quiche s'abîme

_____

8. cela m'ennuyerait/mon poulet rôti perd son goût

_____

F. **Paul est en difficulté.** Paul is having trouble at school. Combine each pair of clauses into a single sentence to find out what he should do to improve.

Modèle   je regrette/Paul ne réussit pas ➤ Je regrette que Paul ne réussisse pas.

1. il est possible/Paul ne sait pas étudier

_____

2. il est important/vous l'aidez

_____

3. ce n'est pas la peine/il perd son temps

_____

4. sa mère a honte/il a de mauvaises notes

_____

5. il faut/il se met à travailler sérieusement

_____

6. il vaut mieux/il fait un grand effort

_____

IV. The Subjunctive after Expressions of Uncertainty, Doubt, and Disbelief

■ The subjunctive is used after these negative phrases that express uncertainty.

il n'est pas certain/sûr que *it's not certain/sure that*

il n'est pas évident que *it's not evident that*

il n'est pas vrai que *it's not true that*

il ne paraît pas que *it doesn't seem that*

ce n'est pas que *it's not that*

Il ne paraît pas que tu **saches** la réponse.	*It doesn't seem that you know the answer.*

■ When these expressions are *not* negative, they are followed by the indicative, such as **il paraît** in the following example.

Il paraît que tu **sais** la réponse.	*It seems that you know the answer.*

■ The verbs **croire** and **penser** are usually followed by the subjunctive when they are negative.

Je ne crois pas qu'il **comprenne**.	*I don't think he understands.*

■ They are followed by the indicative when affirmative.

Je crois qu'il **comprend**.	*I think he understands.*

Because of its meaning, the verb **douter** is followed by the subjunctive when affirmative, but by the indicative when negative.

Il doute que tu **puisses** le faire.	*He doubts that you can do it.*
Il ne doute pas que tu **peux** le faire.	*He doesn't doubt that you can do it.*

G. Ça m'étonnerait. You're skeptical about everything your friends are telling you. Express your doubts using the expressions in parentheses.

Modèle Corinne est de Normandie. *(Je doute que...)*
➤ Je doute que Corinne soit de Normandie.

1. Ses parents sont au Havre. *(Je ne crois pas que...)*

_____

2. Je vais en Normandie. *(Je doute que...)*

_____

3. Joseph a des cousins à Rouen. *(Je ne suis pas sûr que...)*

_____

4. L'oncle de Josette a une ferme. *(Il n'est pas vrai que...)*

_____

5. Nous pouvons visiter la maison de Monet à Giverny. *(Je ne pense pas que...)*

_____

La Normandie

■ Normandy is a rich agricultural region located northwest of Paris and reaching to the English Channel. Normandy's countryside has gently rolling green hills and many dairy farms. The region produces some of France's famous cheeses, such as Camembert. The Seine River flows from Paris northwest through Normandy before emptying into the English Channel.

■ The main cities of Normandy are Rouen, where Joan of Arc was burned in 1431, Caen, and the Channel ports of Le Havre and Cherbourg. The famous impressionist painter Monet is from the little town of Giverny. You can visit his home and see many of the landscapes he painted.

■ In World War II, Normandy was the site of the Allied invasion of Nazi-occupied Europe on June 6, 1944. American and British troops, at the cost of a tremendous number of lives, landed on the beaches of Normandy and broke through the German defenses. By August, 1944, Paris was liberated and the Allied armies fought their way to Germany, liberating France and the Low Countries (Belgium, the Netherlands, and Luxembourg), and defeating Germany in May of 1945.

H. Vos réactions personnelles. Use one of the phrases requiring the subjunctive to express your reaction to each piece of news.

1. Vous avez quatre examens demain.

_____

2. Vous êtes en retard.

_____

3. Vous ne pouvez pas sortir ce week-end.

_____

I. Composition. Write about what you hope your friends will do this weekend (or this summer). Tell how you will feel about what will happen.

END VOCABULARY: FRENCH-ENGLISH

Irregularities of plural formation and adjective agreement are shown in the list at the appropriate entry. Verbs marked *irreg.* should be looked up in the verb charts. Verbs with spelling changes have them indicated in parentheses.

c ➤ ç/a,o: the letter c changes to ç before a and o
g ➤ ge/a,o: the letter g changes to ge before a and o
e ➤ è/mute e: the letter e becomes è when there is a mute e in the next syllable
é ➤ è/mute e *except in future:* the letter é becomes è when there is a mute e in the next syllable, except in the forms of the future tense which retain é
y ➤ i/mute e: the letter y becomes i when there is a mute e in the next syllable

s' **abîmer** to spoil *(of food)*
Absolument pas. Absolutely not. Definitively not.
accepter to accept
accompagner to accompany
acheter (e ➤ è/mute e) to buy
actif (active) active
l' **activité** *(fem.)* activity
l' **addition** *(fem.)* bill, check *(restaurant)*
adorer to adore, love
l' **adresse** *(fem.)* address
l' **âge** *(masc.)* age; **Quel âge as-tu?** How old are you?
l' **agence de voyage** *(fem.)* travel agency
agir to work *(of medicine)*
agréable pleasant
aider to help
aimer to like, love
aîné older, oldest
l' **air** *(masc.)* air
aller *(irreg.)* to go; **aller à pied** to walk, go on foot; **aller en voiture** to go by car, to drive; **Ça va? Comment ça va?** How are you? *(informal)*; **Comment allez-vous?** How are you? *(formal)*; **Je vais bien.** I'm all right. I feel okay.
l' **ambiance** *(fem.)* atmosphere
amer (amère) bitter
s' **amuser** to have a good time
les **anchois** *(masc. pl.)* anchovies
animé lively
s' **animer** to perk up, feel more lively
annoncer (c ➤ ç/a,o) to announce
l' **anorak** *(masc.)* ski jacket
l' **apparence** *(fem.)* appearance
l' **appartement** *(masc.)* apartment
appeler (l ➤ ll/mute e) to call
applaudir to applaud
apporter to bring
apprécier to appreciate *(value, rate highly)*
s' **approcher de** to approach
appuyer (y ➤ i/mute e) to support
l' **après-rasage** *(masc.)* after-shave lotion
l' **arbre** *(masc.)* tree

l' **architecte** *(masc.)* architect
l' **argent** *(masc.)* silver; money
l' **armoire** *(masc.)* wardrobe, armoire
arranger (g ➤ ge/a,o) to arrange
arrêter to stop
arriver to arrive
l' **artiste** *(masc. or fem.)* artist
l' **ascenseur** *(masc.)* elevator
l' **aspirine** *(fem.)* aspirin
s' **asseoir** *(irreg.)* to sit down
assez de enough
attendre to wait for
l' **attitude** *(fem.)* attitude
attraper to catch
au bord de at the edge of, on the shore of
l' **auberge de jeunesse** *(fem.)* youth hostel
autant de as much, as many
l' **auteur** *(masc.)* author
avancer (c ➤ ç/a,o) to advance
l' **avantage** *(masc.)* advantage
l' **avenir** *(masc.)* future
avertir to warn
l' **avion** *(masc.)* airplane
l' **avocat (l'avocate)** lawyer
avoir *(irreg.)* to have; **avoir chaud** to be warm *(said of a person)*; **avoir de la chance** to be lucky; **avoir faim** to be hungry; **avoir froid** to be cold *(said of a person)*; **avoir honte (de)** to be ashamed (of); **avoir peur (de)** to be afraid (of); **avoir raison** to be right; **avoir soif** to be thirsty; **avoir sommeil** to be sleepy; **avoir tort** to be wrong

les **bagages** *(masc. pl.)* luggage
la **baguette** stick, wand; thin French bread
baisser to drop, diminish
balayer (y ➤ i/mute e) to sweep
le **balcon** balcony
la **balle** ball
le **ballon de foot** soccer ball
la **banlieue** the suburbs

le **bas** stocking
les **baskets** (*masc. pl.*) sneakers
le **bateau** boat
　bâtir to build
se **battre** (*irreg.*) to fight
　bavarder to chat
　beaucoup de much, many, a lot of
la **bibliothèque** library
le **bijou** (*pl.* **les bijoux**) jewel
　blanc (blanche) white
le **bœuf** beef; ox
la **boisson** drink
la **boîte** box; **la boîte postale** post office box
les **bonbons** (*masc. pl.*) candy
le **bonnet** woolen cap
la **bonté** goodness, kindness
la **botte** boot
la **boucherie** butcher shop
le **boulanger (la boulangère)** baker
la **boulangerie** bakery
la **bouteille** bottle
la **boutique** shop, store
le **bras** arm
　bref (brève) brief
se **brosser les cheveux, les dents** to brush one's hair, teeth
le **bruit** noise
la **brute** beast

le **cadeau** gift
　cadet (cadette) younger, youngest
se **calmer** to calm down
le **camarade (la camarade)** friend, buddy, comrade
le **cambrioleur** burglar
le **camion** truck
la **campagne** country(side)
le **camping** camping
　canadien(ne) Canadian
la **canne à pêche** fishing rod
la **cantine** lunchroom, student cafeteria
le **capot** hood (*car*)
le **carnet** notebook
la **carotte** carrot
la **carrière** career
la **carte bancaire** bank card
la **carte bleue** French credit card
la **carte postale** post card
la **casquette** helmet
　casser to break; **casser avec quelqu'un** to break off with someone; **se casser la jambe** to break one's leg
la **cassette** cassette, tape
la **cathédrale** cathedral
　Ce n'est pas vrai. Wrong. Not true.
la **ceinture** belt; **la ceinture de sécurité** seat belt
　cesser to stop
le **champion (la championne)** champion
la **chance** luck
　chanceux (chanceuse) lucky
　changer (g ➢ ge/a,o) to change
la **chanson** song
　chanter to sing

le **chapeau** hat
　chaque each
la **charcuterie** delicatessen
se **charger de** (g ➢ ge/a,o) to take care of, to take charge of
le **château** castle
les **chaussettes** (*fem. pl.*) socks
la **chaussure** shoe
le **chef** head, boss
le **chemin** road
la **chemise** shirt
le **chemisier** blouse
　chercher to look for
　chic (*invariable adj.*) stylish
le **chocolat** chocolate
　choisir to choose
la **chorale** glee club
le **cinéma** movies
le **citron pressé** lemonade
le **classeur** loose-leaf binder
la **clé** key
le **colis** package
les **collants** (*masc. pl.*) panty hose
le **collègue (la collègue)** colleague
le **collier** necklace
　Combien (de)? How much?, How many?
le **commencement** beginning
　commencer (c ➢ ç/a,o) to begin
　Comment? How?; **Comment allez-vous?** How are you? (*formal*); **Comment ça va?** How are you? (*informal*)
la **comparaison** comparison
　complet (complète) complete
　compléter (é ➢ è/mute e *except in future*) to complete
　compliqué complicated
　compris included
le **compte en banque** bank account
　compter to count; **compter** (+ *infinitive*) to intend to
le **concert** concert
la **concurrence** competition
　conduire (*irreg.*) to drive
la **confiture** jam
　confondre to confuse
la **connaissance** acquaintance
　connaître (*irreg.*) to know (*people or places*)
　connu famous
le **conseil** piece of advice; **les conseils** advice
　conseiller to recommend
le **consommateur (la consommatrice)** consumer
　contacter to get in touch with
　continuer to continue
le **copain (la copine)** friend, pal
le **coq** rooster
la **corbeille** wastebasket
le **corps** body
　corriger (g ➢ ge/a,o) to correct
le **coton** cotton
le **cou** neck
se **coucher** to go to bed
le **couloir** corridor
le **coup de téléphone** telephone call

le **courage** courage
le **courant d'air** draft
le **courrier électronique** e-mail
le **cousin (la cousine)** cousin
　　couvrir *(irreg.)* to cover
le **crayon** pencil
la **crème** cream; **la crème caramel** caramelized custard dessert
la **crémerie** dairy, dairy products store
les **crevettes** *(fem. pl.)* shrimp
le **cri** shout
　　crier to shout
　　croire *(irreg.)* to believe; **Je crois que oui/non.** I (don't) think so.
le **crosse** hockey stick
　　cruel (cruelle) cruel
les **crustacés** *(masc. pl.)* shellfish
le **cuir** leather
la **cuisinière** stove

　　d'habitude usually
　　D'où? Where from?
　　danser to dance
le **danseur (la danseuse)** dancer
　　davantage more
　　de bonne heure early
　　débarrasser la table to clear the table
le **débat** debate
les **déchets** *(masc. pl.)* refuse, garbage
　　décider to decide
la **décision** decision
　　décourager (g ≻ ge/a,o) to discourage
　　décrocher (le téléphone) to answer (the phone)
　　dedans inside
　　dehors outside
　　déjà already
　　déjeuner to have lunch
　　demander to ask, to ask for
　　déménager (g ≻ ge/a,o) to move *(change residence)*
　　démodé out of fashion
se **dépêcher** to hurry up
　　dépenser to spend *(money)*
se **déplacer (c ≻ ç/a,o)** to move, to move around, to travel
　　déposer to deposit; **déposer quelqu'un** to drop someone off
　　déranger (g ≻ ge/a,o) to bother
　　derrière behind, in back
　　descendre to go down, to go downstairs
se **déshabiller** to get undressed
　　désobéir to disobey
le **dessin** drawing
le **dessinateur (la dessinatrice)** designer
　　dessiner to draw
se **détendre** to relax
　　détester to hate
　　devenir *(conj. like* **venir**) to become
　　deviner to guess
les **devoirs** *(masc.)* homework
le **dictionnaire** dictionary
　　dîner to have dinner
　　dire *(irreg.)* to say, to tell

le **directeur (la directrice)** manager
　　diriger (g ≻ ge/a,o) to direct
la **discipline** discipline
se **disputer** to argue
la **dissertation** essay
la **distance** distance
le **docteur** doctor
　　donner to give
　　donner sur to face
le **dos** back
la **douzaine** dozen
la **droite** right *(direction)*

l' **eau** *(fem.)* water
　　échanger (g ≻ ge/a,o) to exchange
l' **écharpe** *(fem.)* scarf
　　éclater to burst, break, explode
　　écouter to listen to
　　écrire *(irreg.)* to write
l' **écrivain** *(masc.)* writer
　　effacer (c ≻ ç/a,o) to erase
　　effrayer (y ≻ i/mute e) to frighten
l' **église** *(fem.)* church
l' **élève** *(masc. or fem.)* pupil, student
s' **éloigner de** to move away from
　　embêtant annoying *(colloquial)*
s' **embêter** to get/be bored *(colloquial)*
　　emmener quelqu'un (e ≻ è/mute e) to take someone *(somewhere)*
　　employer (y ≻ i/mute e) to use
　　emporter to carry/take away, carry off
　　emprunter to borrow
s' **en aller** to go away, to leave
　　En aucun cas. Under no circumstances.
　　en bas downstairs
　　en général in general
　　en haut upstairs
　　encore more, again
　　encourager (g ≻ ge/a,o) to encourage
　　endetté in debt
s' **endormir** *(conj. like* **dormir**) to fall asleep
l' **endroit** *(masc.)* place
l' **énergie** *(fem.)* energy
l' **enfant** *(masc. or fem.)* child
　　engager (g ≻ ge/a,o) to hire
　　enlever (e ≻ è/mute e) to take off, to remove
　　ennuyer (y ≻ i/mute e) to bore; **s'ennuyer** to get/be bored
　　énormément very much
　　enregistré recorded
　　enseigner to teach
　　entendre to hear
　　entrer to enter, to come/go in
　　envoyer (y ≻ i/mute e) to send
　　épais (épaisse) thick
l' **épaule** *(fem.)* shoulder
l' **épicerie** *(fem.)* grocery
l' **épicier (l'épicière)** grocer
l' **épreuve** *(fem.)* test, quiz; competition
l' **escalier** *(masc.)* stairs, staircase
　　espérer (e ≻ è/mute e except in future) to hope

l' **espion (l'espionne)** spy

essayer (y ➤ i/mute **e)** to try on

l' **essence** (*fem.*) gas, gasoline

essuyer (y ➤ i/mute **e)** to wipe

établir to establish

éteindre (*past participle* **éteint**) to put out

étranger (étrangère) foreign; (as noun) foreigner

être (*irreg.*) to be; **être à l'heure** to be on time; **être à** to belong to; **être d'accord avec** to agree with; **être de retour** to be back; **être en avance** to be early; **être en bonne santé** to be in good health; **être en forme** to be in shape, to be physically fit; **être en mauvaise santé** to be in poor health; **être en retard** to be late; **être en train de faire quelque chose** to be in the process of doing something; **être en vacances** to be on vacation; **être enrhumé** to have a cold; **être grippé** to have the flu

étroit narrow

étudier to study

l' **évier** (*masc.*) kitchen sink

exécuter une ordonnance to fill a prescription

l' **exercice** (*masc.*) exercise

l' **expérience** (*fem.*) experiment, experience

l' **explication** (*fem.*) explanation

expliquer to explain

l' **expression** (*fem.*) expression

exquis exquisite

se **fâcher** to get angry

la **façon** way, manner

faire (*irreg.*) to make, do; **faire des haltères (le haltère)** to lift weights; **faire la vaisselle** to do the dishes; **faire une promenade en voiture** to go for a car ride

le **faire-part** announcement (*wedding, birth, etc.*)

la **farine** flour

se **fatiguer** to get tired

fauché broke (*having no money*)

la **faute** mistake

faux (fausse) false

favori (favorite) favorite

fermer to close; **fermer à clé** to lock

le **feu** fire; traffic light; **le feu vert/rouge** green/red light

finir to finish

la **fleur** flower

la **forêt** forest

fou (folle) crazy

le **foulard** silk scarf

fournir to supply, provide

le **foyer d'étudiants** student center

frais (fraîche) fresh; cool

frapper to knock

le **frein** brake

la **frontière** border

le **fruit** fruit

gagner to earn, win

garder to keep; to watch, to baby-sit

la **gare** railway station

le **gâteau** cake

la **gauche** left (*direction*)

la **générosité** generosity

gentil (gentille) nice, friendly

la **glace** ice cream

la **gorge** throat

le **goût** taste

la **grammaire** grammar

le **gramme** gram (*metric unit of weight*)

le **grand magasin** department store

grandir to grow, to grow up

les **grands magasins** (*masc. pl.*) department store(s)

gras (grasse) fat, fatty

gris (grise) gray

gronder to rumble

gros (grosse) fat, big

grossir to get fat

guérir to cure, to make better; to get well

le **guide** guidebook

s' **habiller** to get dressed

habiter to live (*reside*)

l' **habitude** (*fem.*) habit

le **haltère** weight (*exercise*); **faire des haltères (le haltère)** to lift weights

hésiter to hesitate

l' **hôtel** (*masc.*) hotel

l' **huile** (*fem.*) oil

humain human

l' **immeuble** (*masc.*) apartment house

s' **impatienter** to get impatient

l' **imperméable** (*masc.*) rain coat

l' **importance** (*fem.*) importance

l' **infirmier (l'infirmière)** nurse

les **informations** (*fem. pl.*) news

inquiet (inquiète) worried, restless

s' **inquiéter (é ➤ è**/mute **e** *except in future*) to worry

s' **installer** to move in, settle in

les **instructions** (*fem. pl.*) instructions

s' **intéresser** to get/be interested in

l' **intérêt** (*masc.*) interest

interrompre to interrupt

l' **invitation** (*fem.*) invitation

inviter to invite; **Je t'invite!** My treat!

jamais never; **Jamais de la vie!** Never!

la **jambe** leg

le **jambon** ham

le **jardin** garden; **le jardin public** public garden

jeter (t ➤ tt/mute **e)** to throw

le **jeu vidéo** video game

la **jeunesse** youth

jouer to play

les **jumelles** (*fem. pl.*) binoculars

la **jupe** skirt

le **jus de fruits** fruit juice, **le jus de pommes** apple juice

jusqu'au bout to the end

le **kilo** kilogram
le **klaxon** car horn

le **lac** lake
laisser to let, leave behind; to allow
lancer (c ➢ ç/a,o) to launch
laver to wash; **se laver la tête** to wash one's hair;
    se laver les mains, la figure to wash one's hands,
    one's face
la **leçon** lesson
la **lecture** reading
léger (légère) light
se **lever** (e ➢ è/mute e) to get up
la **liberté** freedom
la **limonade** non-carbonated soft-drink
lire *(irreg.)* to read
le **logement** housing, lodging
loger (g ➢ ge/a,o) to house, to put someone up
long (longue) long
longer (g ➢ ge/a,o) to walk along, to go along
louche suspicious-looking
louer to rent
lourd heavy
le **loyer** rent
la **lumière** light
les **lunettes** *(fem. pl.)* eyeglasses; **lunettes de soleil**
    sun-glasses
le **luxe** luxury; **de luxe** luxury *(adj.)*

la **machine** machine
le **magazine** magazine
maigrir to get thin
la **main** hand
la **maison** house
la **manche** sleeve; **à manches courtes** short-sleeved
manger (g ➢ ge/a,o) to eat
la **manière** way, manner
se **maquiller** to put on makeup
le **marchand (la marchande)** merchant, storekeeper,
    seller; **le marchand de fruits** fruit seller
le **marché en plein air** open air market
marcher to walk; to work, to run *(of cars, machines,
    etc.)*
marron brown *(invariable adj.)*
le **match** match, competitive sports event
la **matière** subject *(school)*
le **médecin** doctor
le **médicament** medication
la **mémoire** memory
menacer (c ➢ ç/a,o) to threaten
le **ménage** household, housework; **faire le ménage**
    to do the housework
mentir *(irreg.)* to lie
le **message** message
mettre *(irreg.)* to put; **mettre la table** to set the
    table; **mettre la télé, la radio, l'air conditionné**
    to turn on the TV, the radio, the air conditioner;
    Je ne sais pas quoi mettre. I don't know what
    to wear.; **se mettre en colère** to get angry;
    se mettre en route to get going, to start out
meublé furnished

mincir to get slim
la **mobylette** moped, scooter
modéré moderate, reasonable
moins de fewer, less
monter to go up, to go upstairs
la **montre** watch, wristwatch
montrer to show
le **monument** monument
la **mousse au chocolat** chocolate mousse
la **moutarde** mustard
le **mouvement** movement
le **musée** museum; **le musée d'art** art museum

nager (g ➢ ge/a,o) to swim
la **natation** swimming
nettoyer (y ➢ i/mute e) to clean
neuf (neuve) new
le **nid** nest
le **niveau** level
ni... ni neither . . . nor
le **nom** name
non plus neither; **moi non plus** neither do I
la **note** grade, mark *(school)*
noyer (y ➢ i/mute e) to drown
le **nuage** cloud
nulle part nowhere
le **numéro de téléphone** phone number

obéir to obey
s' **occuper de** to take care of, to take charge of
s' **offenser** to get insulted, offended
offrir *(irreg.)* to offer; give something as a
    gift
l' **oiseau** *(masc.)* bird *(pl. les oiseaux)*
l' **omelette** *(fem.)* omelette
optimiste optimistic
l' **orage** *(masc.)* storm
ordonner to prescribe
organiser to organize
l' **origine** *(fem.)* origin
Où? Where?
oublier to forget
ouvrir *(irreg.)* to open

la **page** page
la **paire** pair
le **palet** hockey puck
le **panier** basket
le **pantalon** pants, pair of pants
le **paquet** package
le **parapente** parasailing, parapenting
le **parc** park
pareil (pareille) similar
parler to speak, to talk
partager (g ➢ ge/a,o) to share
partir *(irreg.)* to leave, to go away
partout everywhere
Pas du tout. Not at all.
pas encore not yet
pas mal de a lot of *(colloquial)*

passer to pass; to pass by, to go by; spend *(time)*; to take *(test)*

passionnant exciting, interesting

se passionner (pour) to get excited (about)

les patins à roulettes *(masc. pl.)* roller skates

la pâtisserie pastry shop

le patron (la patronne) boss

payer (y ➢ i/mute e) to pay

le pays d'origine country of birth, country of origin

le paysage scenery

la peau skin

se peigner to comb one's hair

le peintre painter

la peinture painting

pendre to hang up

pénible annoying, boring

penser to think

perdre to lose; se perdre to get lost

le permis (de conduire) driver's license

la permission permission

personne no one, nobody

la personne person

peser (e ➢ è/mute e) to weigh

le petit ami boyfriend

le petit déjeuner breakfast

le petit mot note, brief letter

la petite amie girlfriend

peu de little, few; un peu de a little

les phares *(masc. pl.)* headlights

le pharmacien (la pharmacienne) pharmacist

la pièce room

le pied foot; pieds nus barefoot

la piscine swimming pool

la place room, space; la place centrale main square

placer (c ➢ ç/a,o) to place, invest

la plage beach

se plaindre (de) *(irreg.)* to complain (about)

la planche à roulettes skateboard

le plateau tray

plonger (g ➢ ge/a,o) to dive

la pluie rain; sous la pluie in the rain

plus no more; plus de no more, more

plusieurs several

le pneu tire; le pneu crevé flat tire

la poire pear

le poisson fish

la poissonnerie fish store

la poitrine chest

poli polite

la politesse politeness

la pomme de terre potato

le portefeuille wallet

porter to carry; to wear

la portière car door

le pot jar

le poulet rôti roast chicken

Pourquoi? Why?

pousser un cri to cry out, utter a cry

pratiquer to practice

préférer (é ➢ è/mute e *except in future*) to prefer

prendre *(irreg.)* to take; prendre des billets to buy tickets; prendre le petit déjeuner to have breakfast; prendre quelqu'un to pick someone up *(to take him/her somewhere)*; prendre un café to have a cup of coffee; prendre une décision to make a decision

préparer to prepare

présenter to present

le pressing dry cleaner

prêter to lend

le professeur teacher[1]

le programme d'études syllabus

programmer to program

le programmeur (la programmeuse) programmer

le projet plan, project; le projet d'études school project

la promenade à vélo bike ride

se promener (e ➢ è/mute e) to take a walk

la promesse promise

prononcer (c ➢ ç/a,o) to pronounce

prudent careful, cautious

public (publique) public

la publicité advertising

le pull sweater

la purée de pommes de terre mashed potatoes

Quand? When?

Que? What?

Quel(le)(s)? Which?

quelqu'un someone, somebody

quelque chose something

quelque part somewhere

quelquefois sometimes

Qui? Who? Whom?

la quiche quiche, type of soufflé

quitter quelqu'un to leave (someone); se quitter to leave each other, to separate

raccompagner to accompany someone home

raccrocher (le téléphone) to hang up (the telephone)

raconter to tell, tell about, relate

la radio radio; la radio à ondes courtes short-wave radio; le radio-réveil radio alarm clock

la raison reason

ranger (g ➢ ge/a,o) to put away

rapporter to bring back

la raquette de tennis tennis racket

se raser to shave

rayer (y ➢ i/mute e) to cross out

recevoir *(irreg.)* to receive, to get; to have company, to entertain; recevoir son bulletin de notes to get one's report card

la récréation recess

rédiger (g ➢ ge/a,o) to draft, write

réfléchir to think, reflect

refroidir to get colder or cooler

refuser to refuse

regarder to look at

[1]Colloquially, la professeur is sometimes used for a female teacher, especially among students.

la **règle** rule
la **reine** queen
rembourser to pay back
remercier to thank, say thank you to
remplacer (c ➤ ç/a,o) to replace
remplir to fill
rencontrer to meet
rendre to give back, to return
renoncer (c ➤ ç/a,o) to resign, quit
rentrer to bring in (conj. with **avoir** in this meaning)
rentrer to return, to go back, to go home
répéter (é ➤ è/mute e except in future) to repeat
répondre to answer
se **reposer** to rest
le **réseau** network; **le réseau d'espions** spy ring
le **réservoir** gas tank
la **résistance** resistance
retourner to return, come/go back
retrouver to meet (by appointment)
se **réunir** to get together
réussir to succeed
réveiller to wake (someone) up; **se réveiller** to wake up
revenir (conj. like **venir**) to come back
le **rhume** cold; **prendre un rhume** to catch a cold
le **rideau** curtain
rien nothing
rire (irreg.) to laugh; **dire quelque chose pour rire** to say something as a joke; **Et je ne ris pas!** I'm not joking.
le **roi** king
le **roman** novel
rougir to blush
roux (rousse) ruddy, reddish
rester to stay, remain
la **ruine** ruin

le **sac** handbag; **le sac à dos** backpack; **le sac de couchage** sleeping bag
la **saison** season
la **salade** salad; lettuce
sale dirty
salir to make dirty
la **salle à manger** dining room
le **salon** living room
saluer to greet
la **santé** health
la **sauce** sauce, gravy
le **saucisson** salami
le **saumon** salmon; **saumon fumé** smoked salmon
savoir (irreg.) to know
le **savon** soap
scolaire having to do with school
le **sculpteur** sculptor
la **séance** showing (of a film)
sec (sèche) dry
le **sèche-cheveux** hair-dryer
secret (secrète) secretive
le **secrétaire (la secrétaire)** secretary
le **sentiment** feeling
sentir (irreg.) to feel, to smell (something); **se sentir** to feel

le **service** service
la **serviette** napkin; briefcase
servir (irreg.) to serve; **se servir de** to use
le **shampooing** shampoo
le **shopping** shopping
le **sirop pour la toux** cough syrup
les **skis** (masc.) skis
la **soie** silk; **en soie** made of silk
soit... ou either . . . or
soit... soit either . . . or
le **sondage** poll
sonner to ring
sortir (irreg.) to go out
souffrir (irreg.) to suffer
sous la pluie in the rain
souvent often
spacieux (spacieuse) spacious
la **spécialité** specialty
sportif (sportive) athletic
le **stade** stadium
le **stationnement** parking
suivant following
suivre (irreg.) to follow; **suivre le conseil de** to follow the advice of; **suivre un cours** to take a course; **suivre un régime** to be on a diet; **à suivre** to be continued
le **sujet** subject
le **supermarché** supermarket

le **tableau** chalk board; picture
le **talon** heel; **aux talons hauts** high heeled
tant de so much, so many
la **tarte** pie-like pastry; **la tarte aux fraises** strawberry pie; **la tarte aux pêches** peach pie; **la tarte aux poires** pear pie; **la tarte aux pommes** apple pie
la **tartine** slice of French bread and butter
le **tas** pile, heap; **un tas de** an awful lot of
le **tee-shirt** T-shirt
tel (telle) such a
la **télé** TV
la **télécopie** fax
téléphoner to phone
la **tente** tent
le **terrain de camping** campground
la **tête** head
le **théâtre** theatre
la **thèse** thesis
le **tiroir** drawer
les **toilettes** (fem. pl.) toilet
tomber to fall
le **tonnerre** thunder
toujours always
le **tourisme** tourism
tourner to turn
tout everything
tout droit straight ahead
tout le monde; tous everyone
la **traduction** translation
la **tranche** slice
travailler to work
traverser to cross
trop de too much, too many

trouver to find
tutoyer (y ➤ i/mute e) to use the **tu** form to
   someone

l' **université** *(fem.)* university

les **vacances** *(fem. pl.)* vacation
la **vedette** film star
le **vélo** bicycle, bike; **le vélo tout terrain (le VTT)**
   mountain bike
vendre to sell
venir *(irreg.)* to come
vérifier le niveau de l'huile to check the oil
la **vérité** truth
les **vêtements** *(masc. pl.)* clothing
la **victime** victim
vieillir to age, to get old

la **ville** city; **en ville** downtown, in town
le **violon** violin
le **vitre** car window
la **vitrine** shop window
voir *(irreg.)* to see
la **voiture** car
voler to steal
le **voleur** thief
le **volley** volleyball
vouvoyer (y ➤ i/mute e) to use the **vous** form to
   someone
le **voyage** trip
voyager (g ➤ ge/a,o) to travel

le **yaourt** yogurt

le **zoo** zoo

INDEX

A

adjectives
  agreement 87
  comparison 96–97
  gender 87
  indefinite 120
  irregular 88–90, 92–93
  number 87
  position 92, 94–95
  superlative 98
adverbs 189
  formation 194
  of place 192
  of time 189
  position 189, 190, 196
  with the passé composé 196
affirmative counterparts to negative
  expressions 109
aller 45, 207, 211, 219
  aller + infinitive (futur proche) 48
articles
  definite 72, 77–78, 83–84, 190
  indefinite 72, 75–76, 77, 84, 115
  partitive 80–81, 84, 115
  uses
aucun 118, 119
avoir 31, 138–139, 207, 211
  expressions with *avoir* 35

C

ce qui, ce que 186
c'est vs. *il est* 85
connaître 42, 158
  savoir vs. *connaître* 42
commands (See imperative) 160
comparison of adjectives 96–97
conditional 210
conditional sentences 213
contractions 72, 80, 101
croire 65, 138

D

devoir 50, 138, 207, 211
dire 67, 138, 218
direct object (definition) 124–125

E

écrire 63, 138
en 132
-*er* verbs
  present tense 1
  with spelling changes 6

est-ce que 101
être 31, 138, 142–143, 207, 211, 219
  expressions with *être* 36
  imperfect tense of 149–150

F

faire 38, 138, 209, 211, 219
  expressions with *faire* 38–40, 81
feminine forms
  of adjectives 87, 88–89, 90, 93
  of nouns 75–76, 77, 78
future tense 207

G

gender determination by ending
  75–76, 77, 78
geographical names 203, 204–205

I

imperative
  formation 160
  object pronouns with 165
  of reflexive verbs 178
imperfect 149–150
  imperfect vs. passé composé 155
  imperfect with *si* 154, 213
indefinites 111, 115, 120
indirect object (definition) 128–129
inversion 101, 104, 106, 109
-*ir* verbs
  irregular 21
  present tense 12

L

lire 63, 138

M

mettre 61, 138

N

negatives
  negative sentences 111, 115
  negative words 111–112, 118–119
  position of negatives in the passé
    composé 140
ne... que 115
n'est-ce pas? 109
non... plus 118
nouns
  gender and number 72, 75–76,
    77–78, 79–80, 83–84

O

object pronouns
  direct 124–125, 132
  double 135
  indirect 128, 130
  position 124, 128
  with commands 165
on 1

P

partir 25, 55
passé composé
  with *avoir* 138–139
  with *être* 142–143
  of reflexive verbs 174–175
  special meanings of certain verbs
    in 158
past participle 138–139, 142
  agreement 142–143, 145
  formation 138
personne 111, 112
pour + infinitive 199
pouvoir 49, 138, 207, 211, 219
prendre 58, 138, 213
prepositions 198–199, 200–201,
  203, 204–205
present tense
  uses 1

Q

question formation 101
question words 104, 106–107
que (relative pronoun) 182
qui (relative pronoun) 180

R

-*re* verbs 14
recevoir 68, 138, 207, 211
reflexive verbs
  formation 169
  imperative of 178
  in verb + infinitive constructions
    172
  negative 169, 172
  interrogative 169
  passé composé of 174–175
  reciprocal use of 176
relative clauses 180, 182, 186
  agreement of past participle 180
rien 112
rire 68

S

savoir 42, 138, 158, 207, 211, 219
  savoir vs. *connaître* 42
sentir: use of 26
si vs. *oui* 109
sortir: use of 25, 55
stressed pronouns 6
subjunctive 217
  after expressions of doubt and
    uncertainty 225
  with verbs of volition 220
  with verbs of emotion 222
  with verbs of necessity 220
suivre 68, 139
superlative 98

T

time, expressions of 189
tout, tous 121

V

venir 56, 139, 207, 211, 219
  venir de 56
verb + infinitive constructions
  54–55
voir 65, 139, 207, 211
vouloir 49, 139, 158, 207

Y

y 130–131